Being Happier

For Tessa and Oliver

who hold our future in their hands

Acknowledgements

It would be impossible to acknowledge individually all the friends and colleagues who have contributed to this book in so many different ways. Nonetheless, I must thank those many friends in the University of Sheffield, the Open University's East Midlands and Scottish Regions, the Tate Gallery and the BBC, and in particular Jean Allen, Annelene Furness, Ros Hancock, Nicki Martindale, Mhairi McKenna, Lance Moir, Peter Reeves and Estelle Roth, without whose kindness and support this work could not have been published.

For Joyce, with kind regards, [signature]

Being Happier

Colin Roth

Published by Kingfield Press

Printed on acid-free paper in the UK by Cromwell Press Ltd, Melksham, Wiltshire

British Library Cataloguing in Publication Data
A catalogue record for this book is available from the British Library

ISBN 1 901468 00 3

Distributed worldwide by
Sheffield Academic Press Ltd, Mansion House, 19 Kingfield Road, Sheffield S11 9AS, UK

Contents

The Fairy Tower,
Dunvegan Castle,
Skye
11 August 1993

Completed, Loudoun,
The Foreland,
Ballantræ, Ayrshire
16 April 1995

Quantum cedat virtutibus aurum
With virtue weighed, what worthless trash is gold!

S. Johnson, Skye, 13 September 1773[1]

This book is meant to be useful.

That means that some people who read it will be infuriated; I hope that they may be persuaded that it has some value when they see that the ideas it presents work, even if they, like the author, struggle to explain why.

Because the book is meant to be useful, explaining *why* something works is treated as less important than showing *how* it can work.

Because the book is born of an eighteenth century spirit of confidence in the comprehensibility of life and the world we live in, it deliberately eschews notions of 'scientific' proof that emerged during the eighteenth, and have dominated the structure of our belief about knowledge in the nineteenth and twentieth centuries.

The book asserts, and depends upon, the paradox that we experience ourselves both within and beyond the society we live in: we are like each other in many ways, and at the same time absolutely distinct as individuals.

Nothing that is said here about genetic conditioning of personality contradicts the possibility of our being distinct, and having control over the way our lives develop. Indeed, one of the principal conclusions of this book's argument is that our good mental health depends on the vigour and directness with which we exercise control over our situation, and make meaningful choices about our lives' progress. Though what is said may fly in the face of currently accepted belief about our capacity to forge a new personality for ourselves at will, nothing here is more than common sense applied to experience—again, a very eighteenth century approach to understanding—with a profoundly reductionist thought applied to the evidence for the sake of understanding its design.

I believe that the 'elegance' of the ideas presented here—the way that so much seems to make sense if understood in terms of this simple pattern—is the only necessary proof of their truth. The real truth will come later though, if this book succeeds in its aim: helping its readers to 'be happier'.

Understanding why

Everything's appearance depends on where you stand to look at it. That 'appearance' is a subjective expression of the relationship between the viewer and the viewed, rather than an objective reality, has been a principal concern for many of the philosophers whose ideas have conditioned our way of experiencing in the twentieth century. Einstein, Heidegger and Husserl, and others besides, have all stressed that we experience 'reality' from inside it, as ourselves a living and changing element of the reality we seek to understand.

The notion that there was a material difference between subjective and objective experience emerged in the mid-eighteenth century, finding its first conspicuous utterance in Diderot's uncomprehending reviews of paintings by Chardin and Boucher at the Paris Salons of the 1760s.

For Diderot, Boucher's fat ladies were a ludicrous fancy, to be disparaged for their improbability. In a beautiful instance of the phenomenon Freud recognised in jokes, Diderot penetrated the exact truth of Boucher's aim while he sought to make fun of it: 'This is the reality of the imagination', he has the artist say in a mock conversation, as though to admit the role of invention was to damn the artist forever.

Chardin, argued Diderot, captured truth as it was, by painting mundane objects in a rough-textured style which embodied Diderot's sense of the paintings' meanings. That Chardin's work actually contains moral tales, symbols drawn from a traditional iconographic repertoire, and a considerable dollop of eroticism, all aimed firmly at the practical end of selling pictures to a fussy and fashion-conscious market place in France during the 1730s and 40s, slips past Diderot because it is not something he can see from where he stands.

For him, 'reality' in art is where the artist produces an image which is congruent with the critic's experience, not so much in terms of physical appearance but because the *absence* of moral or narrative content—Chardin's intended meanings being invisible from Diderot's standpoint—allows the meaninglessness of 'objects' to be echoed in the apparent meaninglessness of the art.

So, if objectivity is a cultural fiction, a notion invented by pragmatists and exploited by capitalists to excuse their behaviour, and if all experience is subjective, inescapably conditioned by our own interactive perception of it, then we need to seek other lines of view to help us understand our experience.

Our sense of distinctness from our surroundings should not, I think, be displaced. Rather, it should take a useful role in a matrix of perceptions which, by clustering differential experiences against each other, together offer a clearer sense of experience as a whole.

For our culture, in our time, it seems to me that the primary route to understanding our experience of that which is outside us is to ask, 'Why is that done so?' We believe (others may not) that we make choices in all our actions; if we only do things because we have a reason, conscious or unconscious, and if all our behaviour is the manifestation of motivations stemming from interactions between ourselves as individuals and the societal pressures and demands on us, then seeking to understand what motivates the behaviour of others as well as ourselves will generate a dynamic model of *why* we make our choices. That, in turn, will make the dynamics of behaviour and experience comprehensible.

Instead of judging actions by their consequences, a route always impaired by the inadequacy each of us experiences in matching objectives to achievements, let us understand consequences by their motivations, so that imperfect realisation ceases to be a barrier to the satisfaction of need.

Understanding *why* someone undertakes a course of action—understanding why we act ourselves—produces a perceptual model of our wants, rather than our deserts, a clearer guide than 'reality' to the forces which condition, however unsuccessfully, our every gesture.

Being true to ourselves

It has been a central premise of the Judæo-Christian-Islamic tradition that goodness of spirit is manifest as goodness of behaviour; further, that goodness may be measured by a standard exemplified by the founding fathers of these religions. As a consequence our culture has evolved a belief that there is one ideal of good behaviour to which we should all aspire.

The obvious problem that there are, therefore, a much greater variety of ways of being bad, is dealt with more through the power of language than logic: everything which is not 'good' is called bad, and that name gives it uniformity with all else that is not good.

The less obvious problem is that we unthinkingly accept that there are different kinds of good which are appropriate to different classes of people. Our culture believes that the womanness of a woman determines a set of qualities, all perceived in the central model of goodness, in which it is most appropriate she should excel. Equally, for a man goodness is seen in terms of a correlating but distinct set of qualities, also visible in the central model, but held to be appropriate to this gender because of its social function.

In modern times campaigners for one group or another have worked to modify both these, and other models of goodness, arguing that individuals of any gender may legitimately excel in any quality recognised as 'good'. What these campaigners all too rarely recognise is that the problem does not lie in the legitimacy of individualised conformity to the central type, but in the promotion of a central type at all.

Why should goodness not consist of a cluster of moral, social and practical virtues, balanced appropriately for each of us, designed to promote divergence rather than convergence towards a supposedly unitary ideal?

It is a central premise of this book that personal happiness derives from society's helping individuals to develop their own strengths for the personal and general good, while happiness is constrained in a society which demands instead that individuals should give priority to conformity, and only second place to excellence.

If we could aim to capitalise on our strengths, and reject imitative conformity as a merit in itself, the congruence between personal and social aspiration, between personal fulfilment and social good, would be to all our benefits.

It is clear that this is a view which is a product of the late twentieth century. It is a part of the cycle of cultural change which will allow the consequences of Romantic Individualism (that is, more broadly, the Person- as opposed to God-centred focus of Post-Renaissance cultural development) to ease towards whatever social outlook will emerge in the coming century. If, as I believe, we are moving back towards a mediæval-type structure for society which values smaller self-sufficient units and compromise over grand structures and individual genius, then perhaps we might save the best of the past four hundred years' discoveries to contribute to the well being of those living through the coming cycle.

The failure of the mediæval model was that it confined choice for individuals, limiting their potential to contribute to society's growth and well-being. It assumed that long-training and nurture in the family business would produce the best quality.

Post-Renaissance culture absolutely reversed this, most conspicuously in the nineteenth and twentieth centuries, when it was increasingly felt that the best qualities emerged if each individual was allowed to develop with a completely free choice of career. Unfortunately, to be an excellent sports person, you need a body nature has fitted for the purpose, just as to be an academic, you need an easy brain. The aspirational screw which encourages uncoordinated geniuses to aspire to be footballers, and naturally physically adept people to be engineers, produces what may be a statistically similar social consequence to the mediæval model: instead of excelling to the degree that our aptitude suits us to the family trade, now we excel to the degree that our culturally-induced aspirations are congruent with our physical and mental capacities.

Being grateful for what we have

All of us have to come to terms with the most obvious symptoms of natural process: if our parents have red hair, long noses or narrow shoulders, we stand a pretty good chance of having some of those attributes ourselves. We also have to come to terms with any limitations they seem to impose and, as our culture operates at present, still aim to come as close to the cultural norm as we can.

But if we take away the assertion of a central type, and encourage individuals to make the best of themselves, wherever and whatever they are—if we depose the God of Conformity—we can begin to think the unthinkable: that we inherit elements of our personality as well as our physique from our parents.

It is so obvious that we must, and has always been so since Darwin finally forced us to recognise our status as a part of the animal world: we are subject to the same mechanisms of evolutionary change as other animals. Until we discard the belief that nurture is at odds with nature, instead of recognising that they both play important but distinct roles in determining our personalities, we fight against accepting the obvious: the genetic pattern we inherit from our parents conditions the structure of our personality, the matrix upon which nurture seeks to work, just as we inherit red hair and long noses.

What do we have?

If we accept the obvious, that elements which condition our personality are inherited from our parents along with elements which condition our physical being, the immediately arising problem to consider is, which bits of the construct we call personality are heritable, and which are learned and taught?

A good place to start is to ask what we know about the mechanics of inheritance: a theory of personality-inheritance which failed to achieve congruence with known patterns in other areas would strain credulity.

One way of describing the inheritance transmission mechanism, DNA, is to say that it is formed of strings of bipolar switches. The complex interaction of sets of recessive and dominant genes was first recognised by Mendel, and school biology traces the appearance and disappearance of features like blue and brown eyes, hair colour, or long and short ear lobes, in families.

A singular example of this bipolar function is the way in which the chromosomes—each of our bodily cells contains a pair—are either a pair of 'X' chromosomes, or a 'Y' and a 'X'. The process of egg fertilisation, in which the first sperm to swim the course, and use its strength to penetrate an egg, seems to randomise the selection of which pair of generative cells begin the next human life in a way which encapsulates Darwin's dictum that the fittest survive.

Whether the sperm's strength is truly engaged in the process, or whether the process is actually completely random, but understood by us in a way which anthropomorphises the participants, attributing motivation and the 'good' qualities of strength and determination even to this first stage in the life cycle, the truth is that our maleness or femaleness, a difference which radically impacts on our experience of life, is the product of but one tiny choice.

Not just our bodies

If this one choice, perhaps random and perhaps dependent on 'survival' drives in our genetic material, conditions one significant element in our being, we can look to see what other elements of our physical selves might have a bearing on our 'personality' to understand ways in which bipolar choices might impact on them.

An obvious place to look for this is the brain, much better understood now, though still fascinatingly mysterious in its function.

A quality which Betty Edwards[2] recognised in aiming to teach art more effectively, and which workers in other areas of psychological experimentation have observed too, is that the right hemisphere of our brain is active in controlling conceptual and spatial concepts, issues of feeling and sensibility, while the left hemisphere is the powerhouse of cognition and rationality.

If we place a matrix of cultural constructs about goodness across this simplistic description of brain function, we see that the qualities our society calls good in women: gentleness, caring, even perhaps physical competence, are areas in which the right hemisphere of the brain might dominate; while those qualities admired in the male—independence of spirit, intellectual strength, rationality (a quality some used to assume women could not possess!)—are the preserve of the brain's left hemisphere.

If we then allow that the dominance of one hemisphere of the brain or the other might not be conditional on gender, that is, that it is not part of the X+X or X+Y choice, but a separately functioning bipolar switch in our DNA, then we have a model in which some half of us have a brain hemisphere dominance which is congruent with society's aspiration for our personality, and half have the opposite.

The model that has been presented for the structure of this inherited matrix is that one hemisphere of the brain or the other dominates our perceptual capacities in a way that conditions our subjective experience. This dominance of one hemisphere over the other seems to be accompanied by further pairs of bipolar switch mechanisms which condition in turn our inclinations to be active or passive, and to be positive or negative. A further inherited conditioning factor might be measurable in an 'emotionality quotient' scale, and, as will be discussed later, there is some evidence to suggest that we inherit a 'wiring system' which differentiates between each of our three primary senses, vision, hearing and feeling in a way that makes us use these three senses with different degrees of ease as a medium of address between ourselves and the world we live in.

The further this description passes from the central assertion of a physiologically based, and inherited, dominance of one brain hemisphere over the other to other less certain elements of this dominance's governance of aspects of our personalities, the easier it is to argue that the qualities described are learned rather than inherited. Were it not for our culturally-rooted reluctance to acknowledge the place of inheritance in conditioning personality, it might be easy to agree with this view, but there is a such a strong presumption in our culture that nurture, not nature, is the formative element in building our personalities that I believe it is worth considering the possibility that these factors, too, are at least rooted in some physical inheritance even if it is difficult, at this point, to establish exactly how this mechanism might work.

All this sounds highly impersonal, and highly speculative, so let's adopt some humanising language and examine some examples, to see whether experience bears out this hypothesis.

Clingies and loners

The proposition that we need to clarify with examples and real-world language is that 'personality' is a product of the interaction between the environment we grow up in and an inherited matrix including brain-hemisphere dominance, aptitudes, capacities and other conditioning factors which control and affect the way we experience our environment as we grow. Remember that the main thing I am interested in explaining is a bipolar pattern of motivations, not contradicting patchworks of behaviours. In everything said now, what matters is *why* something is done, rather than just *what* is done.

In the description of types which follows, I am using the word 'clingy' to characterise a person whose right brain hemisphere dominates their personality, and 'loner' to characterise a person whose left brain dominates. These descriptions are deliberately anecdotal and subjective, because they are trying to represent how it *feels* to have one kind of motivating direction or the other.

Throughout the book as a whole, I hope that the mesh of interlocking anecdotes will allow a relatively coherent pattern to emerge. The inescapable limitation of what follows is that it tries to describe *why* people make their choices by saying what they *do*. Asking yourself *why* someone might *do* something I describe will help the patterns to make better sense. I will be assuming, in the course of explaining basic patterns, that the three matrices I have suggested (right–left, active–passive, positive–negative) are of equal status as physiologically determined phenomena, not requiring 'proof' now because discussion of their status is best saved until the patterns I'm attempting to explain have been set out.

In experiential terms, the 'clingies' feel as though they have a clear personality which contains some faults which they recognise: their behaviour is motivated by a wish to achieve the greatest possible degree of social integration through explicit acceptance of them with their failings. 'Loners' feel as though they have no particular personality, but suspect the presence of failings they believe they have to hide to gain social acceptance. Where the clingy comes out with faults flying, the loner's instinct is to erect a barrier behind which the possible presence of unidentified but assumed limitations can be disguised.

Clingy people are motivated by a compulsion to engineer and control feeling, either positive or negative, towards themselves, rather than by what other people might regard as 'logical' considerations. The products of their behaviour have consequences for them which are measured in feelings derived from their own experience, not reason: being ignored means not being loved any more, rather than, 'they're busy doing something else just now'. Personal worth is calculated in terms of perceived levels of power over other people's behaviour towards the individual, rather than in terms of 'objective' criteria relating to professional skill, intelligence or physical competence.

This motivation in terms of the prospect of maintaining power over the way other people behave towards them brings a particular quality to the clingy personality's sense of time. They are always looking forward to calculate what needs to be done to manage the next interaction, and they do it in terms of what they have learned from previous interactions. They aim to use all of the knowledge and experience they have gathered to enhance their control over their future.

Loners have an outlook which a computer specialist might term object-related, as opposed to the process-related outlook of the clingy. They see life and relationships in terms of events and experiences which they preserve as 'thumbnail' snapshots, and measure the value of their experiences in terms of their immediacy, variety and intensity. There isn't an *absence* of feeling, but feeling is perceived as a quality attached to and arising from experience, rather than being in itself the motivatory drive. Collecting differentiated feelings is a good reason for having different experiences, but it's the collection of multiple experiences rather than the urge to practice having control over feeling which motivates.

The loner dislikes the clingy's urge to establish security, both emotional and physical, and prefers freedom to move on to new ideas and experiences. The urge to reach out and control the social environment which is so strong in the clingy is paralleled in the loner by a reluctance to be pressured and a determination to avoid being trapped. Where clingies exercise control over their experience of other people by reaching out to control them, loners exercise control by keeping moving, by staying separate, by being unpredictable and by resisting control.

The loner's experience of time is firmly focused on the present: past experience is valued for its variety, rather than as a resource for conditioning the future. The future is often treated as capable of looking after itself, because life, to be worthwhile, must be valued in its present form rather than as a means to an end. The future is a place of risk, valued for the excitement it might bring, but feared for the risks it also carries. The loner's instinct, rooted in their assumption of indistinct but unknowable personal weaknesses and faults, is to avoid looking forward because they assume that they do not have the skills necessary to exercise real control: instead they throw themselves into the present, and trust to 'fate'. For them, planning the future is a defensive strategy.

Clingies, wholly absorbed in their own sense of personal experience, see themselves as acting on other people's perceptions, while loners, focused on other people's experience of them, act on their own behaviour to achieve modification in other people's perceptions of them.

But aren't we all the same really?

In a sense, yes we are: we all aspire to very similar things, like being admired and respected, being cared for or loved, and socially useful conditioning factors tend to make us see those objectives in terms that sound very similar when we express them. The difference between us isn't so much in what we want for ourselves, as in why we believe we want it; and therefore in the way our minds and feelings believe we should best attain our objectives.

In order to be loved, a clingy will behave in one way while a loner will behave in another. Satisfying our objectives effectively often means not just obtaining a 'satisfactory' outcome, but obtaining it through a congruent and comfortable process. Identifying the motivational pattern which we bring to our objectives, and obtaining appropriately congruent responses in terms of process as well as outcome, is a strategy that really works.

By looking at ourselves in terms of our behaviour, we seem very much alike. When we move our viewpoint and ask why our objectives matter to us, why we have chosen to behave in particular ways, the apparent similarities diminish, and the motivational contrasts make a helpfully clear pattern to explain the different reasons we have for behaving in apparently similar ways.

The culturally convenient proposition that we are all alike has truth in it because all of us are aiming to behave in a way that converges towards the norm, for reasons that will emerge later, but our culture, by minimising the differences between us, causes difficulties as well as solving problems. By concentrating on outcomes, and in focusing on the consequences of behaviour, rather than looking at motivation and the intent behind behaviour, we have to interpret 'facts' and 'actions'. It is just as useful, and more interesting because we don't usually do it this way, to interpret the intentions behind actions, worrying less about the 'facts' and whether behaviours succeed in achieving their intended outcomes or not.

Clingy women

So, we begin by looking to see how a right-hemisphere dominated woman, whose inherited personality structure is therefore congruent with social expectations of her, might think and feel. Because it characterises some of the qualities of her motivational urges, let's call her 'clingy', even though that's not the only behaviour pattern she exhibits.

She sees herself in terms of other people's attitudes and behaviour towards her; her own behaviour is designed to condition the way people feel about her, and the way they behave towards her. If she's 'active', she takes positive steps to condition other people's behaviour; if she's 'passive', she manages her own behaviour in a way that she hopes, or finds, has a comparable impact on the behaviour of others. If she's 'positive', then what she aims for is to get people to like her as she is, and is inclined to think the best of them when she can. If she's 'negative', she controls people's anticipated negative responses to her by behaving in a way that makes her feel safe and in control because her own bad behaviour has produced theirs—she has engineered rejection to avoid other people rejecting her; she is inclined to expect the worst of others.

A positive active clingy woman, then, knows her own weaknesses, and tries to get the world to smile on them because she, in spite of those cheerfully borne limitations, does much to help others. She sets out to get people to like her, by doing good things and by being nice. A woman like this under stress becomes unbearably nice to other people, doing good works that aren't wanted or appropriate, and making her friends run from the threat of her well-meaning warmth. Under stress, she finds it difficult to believe that anyone would not like her, and always reads their behaviour towards her in a positive way until its 'real' meaning is inescapable.

A positive passive clingy woman is much the same in her approach, but hopes to be liked without being intrusive. She bears up under stress, not going out to make people like her, but always looking for the good in what other people do. She, too, is reluctant to recognise that not everyone likes her, but because she is passive, she usually manages to avoid being disliked by too many people. She's quite lucky, because this is the personality Western European culture says a woman should have.

A negative passive clingy woman is depressing and depressed, inclined to think that people will find that her faults are too great for her to be likeable, and quietly, miserably convinced that no-one, whatever they say, really truly loves her.

A negative active clingy woman 'knows' that no-one would or should love her, and goes out proving to herself and the world that she's unlovable. She forces emotions out of people so that at least they hate or dislike her with some strength of feeling. By behaving badly, she can preserve an inner conviction of her own essential loveability, feeling that because she engineers rejection, is isn't altogether 'true'.

What the clingy wants, then, is to be in control of other people's feelings about her and behaviour towards her; she knows who she is, has a sense of what her personality is like, and what her faults are.

The single most conspicuous outward sign that someone else is a clingy is that they try to get others to accept them or cope with them in terms of their acknowledged faults.

Loner men

Let's look next at how a left-hemisphere dominated man thinks and feels. We'll call him a loner, because the word sums up some of his most basic urges even if it fails to encompass all the elements of his personality.

A loner makes decisions logically, thinking about what it's best to do, and sees it as a strength of his that his feelings are subordinated to reason. He thinks other people should be sensible too, and therefore has limited tolerance for people who seem to base their decisions on feeling rather than reason. He can't see any particular reason why anyone else should be particularly interested in him, and in normal circumstances doesn't see why he should have any particular interest in anyone else if there isn't a sensible reason for doing so. He lets other people get on with their lives, just as he would like to be allowed to get on with his. Because he doesn't have a particularly clear sense of 'who he is', he often seems quite different to different people, because loners characteristically adapt to the unselfconsciously recognised needs of the person or people that they're with, transforming the way they behave to gain approval from their immediate audience. This apparent inconsistency causes difficulties for some loners, who recognise the absence of one of the socially approved 'good' qualities, a reliable and coherent personality, and for the people who interact with them because they cannot understand what they regard as inexplicable inconsistency.

A positive active loner man sees himself as a strong independent character. He enjoys having fun, and is prepared to tackle new challenges with great enthusiasm. Because going on doing something once you can do it doesn't seem particularly sensible to him, he often loses interest in things once they've been tried: novelty is more interesting as an emotional gain from experience than a sense of having mastered a difficult challenge requiring long-term commitment. As long as other people don't expect long-term commitment from him, he's happy, and great fun to have around. He manages his relationships with other people without being aware that he is doing so: being good company for others is an accidental consequence of the fulfilment of his own desires: so as long as other people are happy with him, he's happy with them. This unselfconsciousness means that he's particularly ill-equipped to deal with emotional stress arising from other people's irrational demands on him, and the reform of this cultural model is the aim of the movement to breed 'new men' (who are actually a different personality group gaining cultural hegemony). This has been the kind of man, strong, independent, sensible, that our culture has trained boys to grow to be.

A positive passive loner man doesn't feel that much different inside, but stays independent by keeping out of trouble. His instinct is that keeping himself to himself allows him to do what he does best. His laid-back disengagement can seem infuriating as it's usually manifested as an emotional coolness that challenges active clingies to action. The passive loner's instinct to keep separate by inaction usually means that he's more aware than an active loner of his impact on other people, and of other people's impact on him. Unfortunately his reason doesn't often help him to understand why other people should want to make emotional demands on him, and he only learns through experience how to deal with these pressures. His natural response is to pull away and try to get on with his own life, as though connection with other people was either unnecessary or actually disadvantageous.

A negative active loner man[3] wants to have fun, because he believes that seeming to be active will stop people challenging him, and because being busy stops the compulsive introspection which plagues him. He thinks everyone should be able to look after themselves as he has to do. If everyone was strong, as he would like to be himself, no-one would feel threatened in the way that he does, but tries not to think about. He thinks other people are out to defeat him, and uses all his skills to keep them away. He suspects that he is himself bad, and that active defence is necessary. He can't see inside himself clearly enough to be sure that he is good and admirable, so fears the worst. He often has a sense that he doesn't really have a personality: at moments of unhappiness he'll talk about 'finding out who I really am'. Rather than be blamed for being bad, he makes sure that he asserts his rights.

A negative passive loner man adopts much quieter strategies to avoid facing what he fears may be the truth about himself, and which he fears other people will see in him, a sort of inherent unlikeability or worse. He believes that the best way to avoid being disliked, which he assumes is the way people would be bound to react to him, is to pull back towards invisibility, hoping to escape notice and therefore condemnation. Rather than provoking difficulty to prove to himself that his defensive systems work, as his negative active loner alternate might, he hides from the risk that any behaviour of his might provoke any response at all, because he assumes that any response to him would be negative. The happiest form this personality can take is quiet resignation—so this is the normal personality for hermits, monks and recluses, as withdrawal allows them to retreat to what feels like the safest minimal relation to other people, and gives a socially legitimised structure to their self-protective isolation.

Loner women

Loner women are in a very difficult situation, because the social construct of what a woman ought to be like is that they will be the centre of a loving family unit, welcoming the dependency of others, and behaving as though the love of other people is the thing they want most. They would actually like to be independent and strong, and fear dependence because they sense that they might be found wanting. They develop strategies to manage the way other people behave towards them which minimise dependency and maximise the potential for independence. Under stress, this personality fears the discovery of suspected but unproven (unproveable) weaknesses, and behaves in any way which minimises the risk of discovery.

For the positive active loner woman, cheerful confrontation is comfortable, as she develops the confidence to believe in her right to act according to her own needs and perceptions despite the strictures of social convention. She goes out to achieve what she feels is her right, and hers has been the most conspicuous gain from the later twentieth century's feminist movement, because it has given her an alternate social construct to identify with.

The positive passive loner woman has benefited enormously from the feminist movement's creation of an alternate social construct too. Although her instinct is to accept 'ordinary' social conventions, the presence of other possibilities and the support of people who believe in her right as a group member to be more independent than the traditional female role would have her, allows her to integrate quietly and comfortably. Loners' characteristic feeling of not having a strongly defined personality of their own is of particular value here, as the positive passive loner woman can quietly conform to differentiated constructs, and seem 'normal' to groups of people who might regard each other as poles apart.

Clingy men

Clingy men are cursed with the problem that their choices are made in terms of feelings, when the society they live in believes that men ought to make choices conditioned by logical thought instead. It's not that they can't, or don't, think, but rather that their objectives in thinking are plans about people and relationships with people, rather than things. A clingy man will go to a party because, or in case, someone (and most likely a particular someone) interesting will be there, where a loner man will go to a party for the experience of the party as such. For the clingy, a party is an opportunity to meet particular people where for the loner, it's precisely the mix of people, the fact that you must move between them and not stay with one in particular, that's exciting and makes a 'party' situation desirable.

Because their behaviour is conditioned by their quest for acceptance, for validation, clingy men's objectives are inescapably social. They aim for material targets like houses and cars because they hope people will admire them or even better, depend on them, for them. Possessing things which other people must be grateful for borrowing or using ensures the clingy man's social position. While a loner man will choose a car to get to work or to have fun in, or in an attempt to define their supposedly ambiguous personality, a clingy man will choose a car that he can take other people to work in, or which other people he knows would prefer to go to work in if they could, or that he can offer fun to other people by having control of.

Under stress

Under stress, clingies' social validity feels uncertain, and their insecurity is often manifested through an obsessive collection of material things other people (and especially loners) can use or admire. For example, a photographer with every lens for their SLR is more likely to be thinking that the loner they want to impress will admire and be jealous of the completeness of their collection than that they will be envious of the quality of a particular image achieved. The completeness is the objective (because it anticipates the challenge that the job [collecting] might not have been done completely perfectly), not what can be done with it.[4] The sad thing about this state of mind is that its solution to 'the problem' is aimed inappropriately: the loner is not likely to care whether a lens collection is complete or not, and will want to know what activity it's for to measure its value. The behaviour is only successful in the sense that it allows a pecking order to emerge amongst the clingies themselves. They compete with each other for the best 'solution' to a problem which is itself a misjudgment. If clingies are to impress loners, they must be better at relaxing and having fun with no eye on the future. To be of use to them, the lens collection's completeness must be satisfying in itself for the clingy.

This failure to recognise the 'reality' of other people's feelings (what those people would say they felt themselves) is characteristic of clingies under stress: their dominance of feelings over reason means that they easily become self-absorbed, projecting their emotions onto others if they think of them at all. Stressed clingies worry about being liked, and about being not liked, but their solutions (by instinct or training) are always addressed to changing their material presence (their car, or the way they dress) instead of to changing the way they are (boring, domineering, or wet). The stressed clingy fails to recognise, because rational thought is more difficult than feeling, that better matching of behaviour to objectives will produce better feeling. The rationality of this process of recognition and matching is inaccessible.

Loners, under stress, would like to disappear, to be 'not visible'. They become more self conscious of the undefined nature of their personality, and more certain that others will 'see through' them and recognise either its absence, or that badness in it whose existence they are sure of but cannot quite capture to describe or place. A loner under stress becomes strikingly rational, believing that all problems can be removed if they can be thought through. Outsiders don't always find their 'thinking' as rational as the loner doing it, but the activity is characterised by a compulsive consideration of options and connections that seem rational to the loner. There's a tendency for feelings to be dismissed as irrelevant or inconvenient, and stressed loners often describe themselves as 'not having any feelings'. They withdraw from company to avoid what they experience as pressure from outsiders to seem worthwhile.

It's characteristic of a loner under stress to experience other people's feelings strongly, and to operate in fear of them. It can be difficult for a stressed loner to distinguish between realities which are rooted in ordinary observation, and realities which are projected and deduced about others' feelings. In other words, under stress a loner has a heightened sense of the importance of other people's feelings, but less capacity to discern accurately what they are; this is a direct contrast to the stressed clingy's loss of contact with the idea that other people's feelings matter at all, and their withdrawal into behaviours that speak of self-absorption. Where stressed clingies feel their own feeling so strongly that they aren't aware of others', stressed loners feel other people's feelings so strongly that they believe their own personality has been suffocated by them. A stressed clingy becomes more obsessive and self-absorbed; a stressed loner becomes paranoid and frightened, sensing a sort of sucked-in vacuum where their personality ought to be.

To draw a pattern from these observations, we could say that a left-hemisphere character who normally thinks first and feels later finds their thinking focused radically on others' feelings, which they experience as a pressure to feel themselves. A stressed right-hemisphere character who normally feels first, feels more strongly than usual, becoming more obsessed about things and relationships; that is they are forced to think more about what they feel. Under stress, then, we become insecure about our command of the activities regulated by the half of the brain we use less well, and are stirred to an uncomfortable and absorbing struggle to control it more effectively. The feeling of being stressed arises not from the external pressures on us, but from the uncomfortable way in which the easier side of our brain is working overtime to manage what it sees as the weaker side. Stress makes our brain hurt.

The valve

These observations of motivational drives and behaviour under stress, and their explanation as a constraint on the ease with which the stronger side of the brain accesses or manages links with the other, find further support when applied to more extreme mental states.

It is my belief that the two 'normal' personality types, when stressed, become the two 'normal' forms of madness, or to put it the other way around, that all our personalities are just like those we describe as 'mad', but in a less pressured state.

Manic-depression, then, is a heightened state of clingyness, in which the pressure to manage other people's perceptions, either by direct contact with them, or through buying things to impress them, becomes so absorbing that 'normal' activities are left with too little attention or time. The characteristic obsessive shopping of the manic-depressive is an interesting example: it feels inside like an activity directed to other people's perceptions, but is usually on a scale that outsiders find astonishing. Buying a 'complete set' to impress others, or a new appearance in the form of a hairdo, makeup and new clothes, actually scares them, and has practical financial consequences for the shopper which only come into focus once the manic self-absorption of the shopping experience has begun to fade.

Any clingy shops to some extent to gain pleasure. Although the practical content of the activity might seem to dominate (buying toilet rolls or detergent), a clingy will choose where to shop, and how much to buy, in terms of a complex range of factors relating to people. Some part of the shopping decision will be about impressing others with good taste: men's insecurity about their ability to choose clothes well has been exploited mercilessly in the last decades of our century, with designer labels like Levi 501 'Red tab' jeans being bought at high prices—almost coincidentally with clothes attached to them—to prove that the wearer has good taste. Another part of the shopping drive is a response to the retail situation. Less obviously in supermarkets than in small shops, the customer arrives possessing power, in the form of latent capacity to spend money, which it is the job of the sales assistant to unlock. A shop is one of the only places in our society where you can go knowing that, however badly you might feel about yourself, or behave, it is the job of the people there to be nice to you. You receive professionally skilled validation substitute, niceness, gratitude, embodied in the thing you buy. For many clingy shoppers, the goods' value is measured at least in part by the remembered quality of the shopping experience in which ownership was achieved.

So, in manic-depression, the shopping becomes exaggerated, compulsive: the warm experiences in shops seem as good (and more reliable) than ordinary ones, and a normal manic-depressive buys more to impress the sales person, as though they can earn more validation from a bigger spend. The things bought all too often lose all their value (once a complete set has been collected), because the value of the shopping, the thing actually bought, is the gratitude of the shop assistant, not the material object which is proffered as a token of the exchange.

In manic-depression, the emotions govern entirely; the personality (the person's sense of self) is strong (manic-depressives do not believe they are someone else, or that they are broken into parts), and other people's sense of what is reasonable seems unreasonable to them. A manic-depressive seems irrational to others because they act according to how they feel. Their ability to use the left side of their brain, the 'rational' part, is greatly diminished. It's quite usual for a manic-depressive person (or a stressed clingy) to lose touch with the ability to control their money, either buying more than they can afford, or losing the ability to tell whether they can afford something or not.

Schizophrenia, on the other hand, is a heightened form of the personality I have described as 'loner'. The left-brain sees all information as equal in status, and open to rational patterns of understanding. Effective evaluation and prioritisation seem to depend on an important contribution from the right-brain, which gives differential weights to various options; it 'feels' relative significance, helping the left-brain's rational process. The loner's openness to all sources of information brings what others regard as a failure to recognise the difference between that which is 'real', which exists in some kind of objective form, and that which emerges from the person's own thought or feeling, and which others would characterise as different in kind ('not real', or 'imagined'). The strict separation of these two realities has not always been so firm: in the mid-eighteenth century, David Hume used an example of his own feelings about the way a play should be acted as 'empirical evidence' for a philosophical argument, giving his 'subjective' experience equal status to other 'objective' data.[5] It's not just that the two kinds of experimental data are treated as equal: it's that they are not treated (as they soon would be) as different in kind. (See passage on Diderot in Introduction, above.) For Hume, his contemporaries and predecessors, there was no such thing as a differentiation between objective and subjective realities.

So the schizophrenic's way of seeing all things as equally real (when others call them hallucinations or visions) is 'wrong' at least in part because we draw an artificial line between objective and subjective realities whose exact placing is culturally conditioned, and which other people have placed differently. However, it's characteristic of the schizophrenic to find some of these 'real' experiences threatening or fearsome, so that dislocation from other people's sense of reality is compounded by an inner fear of things other people do not believe are 'true'.

The loner's characteristic experience of time in terms of the present, not the future or the past, means that the schizophrenic is cut off from the comparative standard which the rest of us use to calm fears: when children experience the dark, they might 'see' monsters in the shadows. As they grow older, they gain confidence that a room empty of monsters when the light is on will not be filled with them at the touch of a switch. The change in the child's perception is not born of an improving sense of reality, but of an improving command of the construct of memory and prediction, allowing the remembered security of the illuminated room, and the confidence of its re-emergence next day, to command the dangers of the night. Because the schizophrenic's capacity to remember and predict is constrained (for I am suggesting that thinking and experiencing 'now' are left-brain activities, while remembering and imagining or predicting are right-brain ones) their present experience cannot be softened by memory or expectation because their mental life is cut off from access to their right-brain skills. It is this isolation from the past and the future which is responsible, too, for the 'split personality' which so rarely occurs but dazzlingly characterises schizophrenia in the popular imagination. A shift in mood makes a schizophrenic 'be' who they are in it, and it's hardly surprising to find them characterising their moods, or personality facets, with names and qualities in an age obsessed with individuality and personal identity. Schizophrenics' experience of the world is coloured by their perceived failure: they are not a 'person' in particular. Becoming 'somebody' certain, and the becoming somebody else, is a way of reconciling how they think they are meant to be with who they feel they really are. Coming to terms with not needing to have a single coherent personality, and experiencing the shifts in mood as proper parts of a single life, require a command of memory and imagination: schizophrenics need their right-brain function to return to health.

If, then, we are saying that stress on 'normal' people makes them have greater difficulty of access to the functions of their 'weaker' brain-side, and if we are saying that the characteristic symptoms of more extreme mental difficulty suggest one brain-side having to govern all functions, with a clear pattern observable suggesting which side is 'on' and which 'off', then a very simple model of the physiology of stress and madness emerges.

If we posit a 'valve' between the two sides of the brain, we are supposing that someone 'normal' will have behaviour motivated by their 'home' side and readily conditioned by their 'away' side. Someone under stress finds the valve between their brain-sides stickier: their 'home' side works as well as usual, but it's more difficult to achieve a balance, so the clingy is a little more obsessive, and a little more tied to feeling, while the loner is more rational, more interested in the present, less patient with ties to the past or plans for the future.

In 'madness', the valve gets jammed entirely, trapping its owner on one side of the fence or the other, incapable (or nearly so) of emerging towards our averaged life because of the dominance of feeling or thinking, and especially of past and future or present.

If this model is right, then the solution to both stress and madness is the same, and doesn't depend at all on anyone's subjective experience of their life: all that is needed is a freeing up of their valve, so that a 'clingy' can organise things instead of being trapped in feeling, and the 'loner' can remember and compare now with then, so that the difficulties or excitements of the present are less pressing.

Although it may be that there are chemicals (or activities) which help free a valve better from one side than the other, this proposition argues that *any* therapy for stress or madness has to have the effect of freeing up the valve to work—and that only this effect of the therapy matters very much.

My experience of working with schizoid people suggests that getting them to feel anything (by drawing, by playing a musical instrument, or perhaps just holding a hand) quickly limits the scale of their entrapment on their left side. My manic acquaintances equally find themselves less stressed when they are encouraged to be *really* obsessive, not just completing their collections of lenses, but organising the lenses and planning how to use each one. Enforced thinking for the manic personality, enforced feeling for the schizoid, open up the 'away' side of the brain, and practice in using both can gradually restore 'normal' function.

Schizoid personalities can gradually learn to recognise 'special' reality as different in kind to 'ordinary' because it has a quality of freshness and brilliance, entirely desirable, which they can enjoy for its own sake without confusing it with boring bits of life like going to work or relating to people. Similarly, a manic personality can be helped to take on the present, instead of playing for the future, living for now and not just in case, so that shopping (for example) is only allowable if you're actually hungry and haven't any food, or cold and haven't any clothes. 'Reasonable' judgements about long term needs become accessible as the height of empassioned panic about the future is reduced.

Of course this model of what is happening when we're stressed or mad, and of what happens when we tackle those states of mind, has radical implications for the plethora of treatments and therapies which have burgeoned in our century. It explains why, for example, Freudian therapy (what he used to call the 'talking cure') works so well in some ways, but doesn't work better as time goes on. The therapist is helping the client rock their valve during a session, but only gradually easing its use in general because of a misleading emphasis on the importance of 'content' and the past, so that 'manic' patients respond much better than 'schizoid'.

Expectations

A clingy lives now in terms of what will happen soon: life is a sequence of rope bridges suspended hopefully towards a future which is planned as though predictable. The failure of a bridge *feels* more or less dreadful, but no matter how bad the disappointment when a plan fails, if a new bridge can be suspended from the failure towards a new future, the feeling of failure disappears. A clingy will suggest, let's say, a meal at their house to a friend—they like nesting, spider-like, and drawing friends into their web to confirm their ownership of them. It's not unusual for the friend not to be as clear as the clingy that the plan has been made; one of the most frequent disappointments for a clingy is to find that their own vagueness has allowed others to not take a 'plan' as a definite arrangement. 'Why don't you come round for tea on Sunday?' is heard by a loner with the unspoken but to them obvious condition, 'if nothing else more interesting turns up'. The loner cannot understand why the clingy has spent hours and pounds on elaborate preparations for what, to them, was only ever a vaguely conditional arrangement.

Loners don't very often invite people to their homes for tea. Their idea of a good time is to go out with a friend to share an experience. Their home is a hiding place, a retreat, from which they emerge to engage in life. Seeking everlasting variety and renewal, they sometimes seem impatient with the inescapable reality, that if some of life is to seem thrilling and extraordinary there must necessarily be parts which by contrast seem dull and boring.

I therefore want to suggest that part of the differentiation between clingy and loner can best be described *not* as a direct reversal, magnetic style, of poles, as suggested earlier, but as a multi-dimensional contrast. The clingy's world exists in terms of past and future—the present is only a bridge between the two. The loner's world exists now, and is measured outwards from the inner self—the scale goes from destruction (negative inward stress), through dull and boring towards thrilling, in a line which embodies depth and complexity of experience in the present alone. Although a happy loner knows about the past and the future, only now really matters. The complementariness of the relationships between clingies and loners is a function of the contrast in their experience of time: outwards and inwards in the present, or in a line from the past towards the future. The conflicts in relationships arise not from misunderstandings about content (inadequately clear appointments, for example) but from the intrinsically tangential nature of the two personalities' perceptions. There is little a clingy can say to a loner to have them appreciate just how important it feels to them to know that commitments are secure; there is, equally, little a loner can say to a clingy to explain why the *idea* of commitment is so unproductive, because there is no way of knowing what the future will bring.

Behavioural convergence:
Getting it together

We began by contrasting (and criticising) our culture's assertion of a single model of goodness to which all should aspire, with the biological reality (I am claiming) of contrasting polar patterns in our personalities which generate complex interrelationships between gender, brain-side dominance and other factors.

Just as it's difficult to be clear how far those factors are the work of nature or nurture, so it's unclear how far our tendency to behave in an averaged way is a product of social conditioning.

But let's look at what we've been saying about the way that stress operates on our personalities. Although we are motivated by drives which are characteristically left- or right-brain ('don't come too close' or 'please come closer'), we have seen evidence that people feel disfunctional (stressed) or find it impossible to engage with ordinary society (are 'mad') when their brains' functions are progressively constrained to their 'home' side. In other words, to be 'happy', we need to be able to access the skills and experience which are only open to us through our 'away' brain-side, even though our motivations, the patterns of perception which condition the meanings we attribute to our experience, are 'home' based.

That means that balance in access to both brain-sides, a functioning 'home and away' structure, is a definable state of 'normality', a condition to which we ought to aspire. The balancing of elements, the averaging of functions and reciprocity of skills, and especially the promotion of mental health through regular use (and therefore maintenance) of the valve, is demonstrably good for us. Our culture has, without having read this book, evolved a pattern of behaviour which encourages its members to conform to these 'rules' in order to achieve mental health through balanced mental activity.

The *way* in which our society aims to achieve and maintain this balance for individuals, though, is itself the source of much of the stress and disfunction which ails us. Simply behaving (copying behaviour) in an average way does no good at all. What matters is not what we do, but how we do it. Each of us needs a balance between thinking and feeling, between now and then, which keeps our brains in their best state. Behaving in a particular way because we ought to, without reasoning and feeling why, is useless. Here, in truth, is the solution to the old philosophical problem of freedom of will. That has been misunderstood because it has always been taken to refer to an individual's behaviour. But freedom of will is actually a description of the necessity, for our mental health, of taking decisions for ourselves, using both sides of our brain to achieve a special kind of personal independence, or mental self-sufficiency. The average behaviour our society encourages, and which we mostly aim to achieve, is only constructive to the degree that individuals can choose to participate; so the more complex the structure of their individuality (that is, the less they conform to a single model for conformity's sake) the better. To the extent that conformity imposes behaviour and diminishes individuals' needs or desires to make their own choices, our mental health is compromised and our sense of happiness or ease diminished.

Elegance

Our brains are tremendously effective operators: the economy with which the same mental process is applied to different ends is really quite extraordinary. Because our culture is so obsessed with material ends and behaviour, rather than process and intention, it has largely failed to recognise how many widely separated functionalities are the product of identical mental process.

When we watch a rugby match, if possible at Murrayfield, we enjoy it most if we add to our narrative expectation (wondering what will happen, who will do it, when) a knowledge and understanding of the game sufficient to allow us to enjoy *how* the game is played. To get the most out of the experience, we need to know the rules of the game so that our æsthetic appreciation of how the game is played can colour the linear screw of its unfolding story. In terms of our brain patterns, this involves the necessary activity of both right and left hemispheres for the best result for us.

When we look at pictures, or listen to a piece of music, we use exactly the same mental process, making our choice of art form according to which of our senses allow the most immediate visceral experience. We have an interest in what will happen, in the story of the art, and we are engaged in the narrative by the feelings which arise in us as a product of its manner of telling.

Norman Bryson has explained, in *Word and Image*,[6] how at different times in cultural history the primary expressive strategy of art has been either its narrative or its æsthetic component. He points to didactic mediæval art to show how strongly the story is placed at the front of our perception, only then allowing emotional glosses (like the grandeur imposed by the art's scale) to condition our understanding. By contrast, an abstract expressionist painting by Mark Rothko begins with feeling, then invites us to have an experience which we seek to understand by evolving a personal narrative (not necessarily a story, but a rational understanding of the way the painting works, and of its meaning for us) by way of explanation. All art, in other words, seeks to prolong our contact with it, either by getting us to feel in response to a story, or by getting us to seek an understanding of the meaning of our feeling. Some art asks us to stay with the image for a long time, gradually coming towards an understanding of its elements or its function. Some art invites us to do little more than register its immediate impact: its life is in our head later. This 'one-strike' strategy, characteristic of pop art as well as the abstract expressionists to some degree, has evolved partly as an artist's response to our over-paced lifestyle, and partly as a way of coping with our means of selecting experiences from the huge variety available to us in our culture, with its all-pervasive reproduction of all art from everywhere, in which strength of immediate impact has been more highly prized than length of enjoyment. In terms of our brain patterns, clingy art requiring time has given way to loner art which generates depth and exists in the present.

The function of art in our society was described perfectly by Wordsworth in the 1802 Preface to his and Coleridge's *Lyrical Ballads*.[7] He recognised that the artist presents us with a way of having a strong feeling, focused on an object, about which we then articulate our feelings. The function of art in society is to allow us to practise being sensitive, and then to practise articulating our feelings, communicating how we feel to and with others.

These skills then apply to all the other social and personal activities which require the same balancing of narrative and æsthetic or emotional qualities, the same capacity to understand the pattern of a narrative and to develop a mental perception of it that prioritises its elements and comes towards an understanding of its meanings at its various levels, and which can absorb and comprehend the significance within this narrative structure of the ever-present æsthetic or emotional conditioners which impact on all its elements and levels. Our whole social intercourse, our political and economic lives, require these skills, and it is clear that art is not the only human activity whose function is to allow us to practise them. Although the huge variety of the arts, from theatre to poetry, from sculpture to dance, allows most people an opportunity to learn these skills away from 'real' problems, there are some people for whom the arts do not speak, and who use other social activities like sport or good works to perform the same skill-practising role. The skills we learn are 'transferable' between our intimate and our social lives, and all of us function better in society if we have a carefully structured opportunity to develop them.

Our wiring

How far it's something we learn, and how far it's something we're born with a leaning towards (as with so much else discussed in this book) is unclear, but by the time we've started learning seriously, we each have an established pattern of sense primacies which condition our learning strategies. I came across the idea in Richard Bandler's and John Grinder's *Frogs into Princes*,[8] where it's presented as the useful product of observing and learning to work better with hypnotic subjects. They assert that a better rapport can be established with a subject if the therapist takes note of whether that subject sees, hears, or feels most easily, and recognises, too, which of the three senses the subject normally uses second and third.

Bandler and Grinder say that each of us has a pecking order of senses, with the first most receptive, the second having a sort of 'check' function, and the third less easy and regular in use. Further, they say that there is a visible outward sign of this pattern in the way our eyes move when we withdraw from eye contact with a questioner to think about our answer. If we formulate our answer visually (that is, we work out our response in images), our eyes go upwards while we are thinking. If we think in sounds, they go to the side, and if we think 'kinæsthetically' (in feelings) they go down. Each of us uses one sense most of the time as a first resort, and usually checks our thought with the same 'secondary' sense before answering, whatever the 'logical' sense content of a question might be.

So, someone whose visual sense was strongest would, when asked what they had for breakfast, withdraw from eye contact to think; their eyes would go upwards, and then flick briefly either to the side or downwards (depending on their usual pattern) before answering. When asked to talk about what had been in their mind while thinking of their answer, such a subject would confirm that they had 'looked' at their breakfast, or seen themselves eating it, or had some other visual route to memory.

Someone whose first sense was hearing would move their eyes to the side first on being asked the same question, then briefly move either downwards or upwards. Their mental 'image' would be a sound, perhaps the 'snap, crackle, pop', or a name, or the voice on the radio while they were eating. A primarily kinæsthetic subject would think of the taste or the texture of their breakfast, or its smell, or who they were with or where, and their eyes would go downwards first.

In each case, the content of the mental image would be modified to some degree by the individual's secondary sense: a vision-first, feeling-second person might 'see' the breakfast, and then confirm the image with a taste, texture or smell before giving an answer.

An additional layer of signalling makes this pattern even more interesting: when remembering, we move our eyes to the side of our strongest hand (the one with which we write for preference), and when imagining, to the side of our weaker hand.

This phenomenon makes it extraordinarily easy to tell when someone you know a little is lying to you, because a lie is characteristically a remembered (worked out in advance) answer when a spontaneous one is required, or a made-up one when an actual memory (of putting out rubbish, or doing homework) is needed. Once you've asked someone a 'bearings' question, to establish right or left-handedness, their veracity can be assessed all too easily. Coincidentally, this observation provides a linguistic echo of my earlier point about the significance of process over content, and suggests that some of our moral judgments have a congruence (to say no more than that) with patterns in our physiology. By defining a lie as the application of a wrong strategy, you clarify what it is we object to in lying: misinformation (wrong fact) is far less important than misbehaviour (not having done a piece of work, or not being prepared to be spontaneous).

Each of us has a sufficiently idiosyncratic physiology to make the skill of reading these signals a little (and only a little) difficult. For example, the visual up is always to one side or another, but may be only just over the horizon, which can make it look confusingly like 'hearing'. When any of us is under pressure, for example at the outset of an interview, there's a tendency for our eyes to reflect our immersion in feeling by going down first, whatever our normal primary sense. Watching tapes of interviews makes this pattern, and the point at which a subject relaxes to their normal pattern, readily visible. Clearly this pattern is easiest for visual people to see; there are cognate patterns in sense and hearing that can be recognised, but none that I have spotted which is so systematic and obvious as the semaphore of the eyes. It may be difficult to be sure what we mean when we say that our eyes are a window on our 'soul', but there's no doubting that they say a very great deal about what's going on inside us.

Using our senses to learn

Good effective learning seems to take place when we take in information and ideas through our primary sense system, and confirm ownership with our second. Information and ideas that are offered to us in a medium that either demands the use of the third or second senses (that is, excludes the primary) are not taken in as effectively, either because the third and second senses are less effective media for us, or because we attempt to translate incoming material into our primary sense system, having some difficulty doing so with our secondary sense, and rather more difficulty with our tertiary.

As all of the possible combinations of the three senses seem to exist, it would be interesting for a 'scientific' psychologist to conduct experiments to 'prove' these patterns. My own understanding of them comes only from experience of teaching and learning with a very wide range of adults and children, and across an equally wide range of academic and technical disciplines (musicology, art history, history, literary criticism, philosophy, psychology, computing, design, instrumental performance, ballet, skating, photography...).

Let's look at some model instances. Let's suppose that someone who is primarily visual and secondarily kinæsthetic (eyes up first, and check down second—the commonest pattern, in my experience) goes to a lecture at college. If the lecture is entirely aural (spoken), our subject has relative difficulty in getting much out of the event. They have to concentrate hard on listening, and are inclined to write down, in notes, as much of what they hear as they can, because they have learned through experience that they don't remember things said to them which they don't write down. Unfortunately, while they're writing, and looking at what they've written, it's almost impossible for them to hear what's being said, so that their note of a spoken lecture is almost entirely random in its 'sampling' of the data-stream: a piece of information will only be noted if it comes to the surface at the point when this particular individual has finished writing their last note.

Lecturers can (in a better strategy for teaching than just talking) manipulate this process by highlighting significant elements of the contents of their lectures with visual signals—verbal emphasis is missed surprisingly easily. (I experimented with a group of students at the University of Derby in 1994: I told them [but avoided writing down] that the period's pervasive concern for empiricism was the key to understanding cultural development in the mid-eighteenth century— only one student from a group of twenty used the word in the essay written immediately after the session. All the other essays were cobbled together from summary text books about the period I had *said* should be used cautiously.)

The kind of visual signal which defeats this learning problem might be a handout of significant terms, facts or ideas, or a reading list highlighting significant issues. A better signal is for the student to see the lecturer writing key words on a board. The reason this works effectively for our specimen student is that the visual cue is confirmed by an empathetic tactile content. As the student's best learning line is to confirm visual learning with physical activity, seeing information presented visually through a physical action creates a strong congruence between learning skills and teaching strategy. Virtually the same approach works well, for the same reason of principle, for a student who is primarily kinæsthetic and secondarily visual: their tactile response to seeing writing (and copying it themselves) is confirmed by the sight of the written content.

A specimen student whose primary sense was hearing would have been entirely happy with the lecture in its original form, speech alone. They might have taken confirmatory notes to draw in either feeling (writing) or seeing (reading) to back up their memory of the heard and spoken. Their most effective confirmation of their learning, though, would be to talk about the content of the lecture immediately afterwards. The people who come to talk to the teacher after a class will normally be 'aural' and quite often the 'clingy' ones, seeking a double affirmation of their hearing through speaking, and of their commitment to learning through a display of their enthusiasm to their teacher. Aural people might pick up handouts, but don't often read them; diagrams, unless their secondary sense is visual, leave them foxed.

Reversing the learning situation, though, also inverts the relative strengths of the two model students.

If you give both a book to read, the highly visual student has very easy access. He or she can readily absorb facts, analyse arguments and follow patterns of thought while reading at considerable speed. It's usual practice in preparation for higher school exams and degree exams in literature to tell students to read their set books several times. For the highly visual student, this is no problem, and each reading produces new insights and information which had remained hidden in earlier, skimmed, engagements with the text. Visual students like using transparent colouring pens on their texts, to make rapid return to 'significant' elements of the text even more rapid, and allowing a simplistic affirmation in memory through use of their secondary (kinæsthetic) sense.

Primarily aural students find these highlighter pens a real barrier to reading: the colour glares off the paper, making it impossible to see the areas not highlighted, and apparently ruling out anything not so marked as inescapably *in*significant. They don't recognise that for a highly visual person, the marks' impact on legibility is far less than it is for them.

Our aural students can only read at speaking speed. They literally read out loud to themselves, even if they don't make a noise. As long as they don't try to rush, they only need to read their set books once, possibly marking significant elements with grey pencil marks that are barely differentiated from the colour of the text they read. Where their access to spoken information is highly efficient, they struggle with print: it has to be converted to be useful, either in a tutorial discussion, or as a written essay which allows their second sense to confirm the material for them. Unconverted reading sinks without trace.

Primarily kinæsthetic students have the most urgent difficulties at a much earlier stage in their learning cycle. Because doing things, feeling them, is their main way of learning, these students are good at craft and technology skills, and much less good at subjects taught visually and aurally. It's not that they can't achieve success in other subjects, but their learning process has to be routed through their primary sense if it's to work well, and with the same efficiency as other students'.

In the sixties, a lot of clever educational psychologists came to the view, as far as I can tell because their statistical evidence from experiments suggested it, that 'old-fashioned' teaching strategies for reading and writing skills were inefficient. They found that the greatest quantity of successes could be achieved most quickly if reading and writing were taught through a combination of verbal and visual methods, with recognition and reinforcement shared between the two senses. The out-of-date insistence on the simultaneous development of good, or at least neat, handwriting was regarded as an unnecessary burden on young children, who could easily be encouraged to be neater later. This change was made without any recognition that there was a whole class of children, those whose primary sense was kinæsthetic, whose access to reading and writing skills would be entirely cut off if the time given to *their* primary learning route was diminished, and in most schools cut off altogether. To make matters even worse, not just for the kinæsthetic kids but for the aural ones too, a silly graphic alphabet was introduced (the Initial Teaching Alphabet) which meant that visually alert children were given a (for them) easy ride into reading through a simplified graphic presentation of words, while aural children had to pass through a double visual barrier, doing their most difficult learning, of a visual construct, twice. The concentration on the visual element of reading through a simplified alphabet, whose temporary nature must have made it seem even less important to teach handwriting at this early stage, left the non-visual children stranded. We call the result of this dreadful unbalanced teaching dyslexia, but it's certainly not the same thing as 'genuine' dyslexia: it's just the product of shoddy teaching.

To summarise: all of us learn most readily through *one* of our three main senses, vision, hearing and feeling. Each of us confirms that learning, and can also learn reasonably effectively, through our secondary sense, the one of the three that we use to 'check' when we've been asked a question. All of us have greater difficulty in learning through the third sense of the three. This pattern has huge behavioural consequences which will be addressed later in this book. For now, let's recognise that good teaching must allow everyone access to *two* mutually supportive lines of communication; that those two lines will be in different combinations for different individuals; that, therefore, unless the teaching is directly focused on the needs of a single individual, all teaching *must* include access through all three senses if it's to be equally available to all members of its audience.

Defining intelligence

Our century has been plagued with the urge to quantify and measure, and in Britain in the eighties and nineties, there has been a particularly malevolent urge to manipulate expenditure 'efficiently' (that is, without more cost to the ruling class through higher tax rates for higher income earners) in terms of 'measurements' of almost every human activity. Were it not for the effect of these wicked machinations, we might have been happy to let the counters count, and simply ignore them. As it is, the social consequences of their miscounting are too great to be ignored, and the inadequacy of their system needs to be tackled.

So far as measuring 'intelligence' goes, the most obvious malfunction in the system usually adopted is that it is designed to measure visual acuity, rather than general intelligence. Highly visual students with weaknesses in hearing or feeling pass with high marks, while those for whom vision is the weakest sense do badly, no matter what their 'intelligence'! We draw lines in our society around the idea that 'feeling' people are stupid, only good for handicrafts, when actually it's our fault if they have problems because we teach them so badly. We assert that some people are cleverer than others because they read more, when in fact they only read more quickly. Unfortunately it doesn't really take much 'common sense' to recognise that people who read a lot can be remarkably stupid, or that people who aren't terribly well read but are good with their hands can have great insight and intelligence for all their lack of formal learning.

So, let's try and develop a model of intelligence which makes better sense of our ordinary perceptions and allows a greater level of complexity, recognising other skills besides reading-based ones as having value, and giving a clearer picture of our strengths than the present dreadfully misleading system.

Let's say that intelligence is a function of the ease with which an individual learns, and uses what they learn. Each of us has (without asking whether our skills are given, or can improve with practice, or deteriorate with neglect) a separate degree of ease with visual signals, aural signals and kinæsthetic ones. That means that, according to our observations about the three primary senses and their significance in learning, intelligence will need to be measured, for any one individual, in three distinct ways: measuring the ease with which we can use each of our three senses; and measuring the ease with which we convert material between the three senses. Some of us are better at using what we've learned than others, so that needs measuring too, in tests tailored to recognise the different skills of different subjects. Let's have a look at some examples to show how these things work.

A doctor is expected to be able to recognise and remember how to deal with a huge variety of mechanical breakdowns in our biological mechanism. The information doctors have access to in recognising is visual (looking at a patient, or their symptoms), aural (listening to noises, or to what the patient says) and kinæsthetic (feeling lumps and bumps, or smelling them). All this data has to be correlated and readily compared to a mental database assembled in years of study. It's particularly important that a symptom recognised through one sense (an aural manifestation of pain) should be readily connected to others (a visual memory of pain referral patterns in the body, perhaps). Therefore medical students are quite properly selected to be pretty good at all three senses, and especially to be very good at using all three in tandem, easily transferring data between them. Whether it's purely a consequence of their training's emphasis, or a characteristic of their intelligence pattern, it has to be noted that doctors are notoriously bad at *communicating* in a system other people can access, although they are required to be good at *learning* through those systems. They are, characteristically, equally good at all three senses systems, have good recall of information learned, are extremely effective translators of incoming data between all three sense systems, and dismal outputers of coherent information, rarely possessed of the interpersonal skills so prized by others.

At the other end of the spectrum, let's take a car mechanic (not all that far removed from a doctor really), who needs to assemble a pattern of understanding of a car's problem from data which might arrive, like a patient's, in any or all of the three sense systems. Luckily for mechanics, they can ignore everything except the car itself, because they are only judged on whether the car works or not after they have seen to it: the car's family's feelings are less important than a patient's family's because 'repeat purchase' depends on effectiveness, rather than quality, of care. Grumpy car mechanics are less of a problem than grumpy doctors. If they have low access to visual or aural information (how often has your car gone to a garage, and been returned with only part of the work completed, even though the jobs were listed on the note you took with you?) it doesn't really matter as long as the car now works. With output too, as long as the machine works, the rest is irrelevant. Car mechanics can take years to learn the trade without inconveniencing anyone except themselves, so their learning efficiency is not a problem, and as long as they have the practical (kinæsthetic) capacity to do their job, they earn a respectable place in society. The truth is that they do pretty much the same job as a doctor, though often with even less effective communication, and maybe a little slower because cars don't die in quite the same sense that people do.

Good musicians must, in the end, be good doers, but they can't do well enough if they can't hear, so they need good linkage between kinæsthetic and aural senses, but have very little need of vision. That's why good musicians always (nearly always) will tell you that they struggle with reading music, and why the ones who read it most effectively (the critics) can't do it very well!

A good dancer, or artist, needs great control of the kinæsthetic, with the same capacity to call on vision that the musician must have of their aural sense. Good dancers learn something from being shown, and from looking in mirrors, but they learn a lot more from their teacher's touch, a stroke along the line of a thigh or arm, or a touch on the hips to correct their stance. Just as the good musician moves from a visual and aural set of sources (seeing the notation, hearing how other people do the same thing) towards a secure physical control of their own actions in *making* music, so a dancer moves from visual sources (watching others and seeing themselves) and a small aural component (the teacher's voice, the music they dance to, whose rhythm's 'feel' is usually its most accessible element) towards a secure physical control of *their* activity. For both musicians and dancers, one sense is hugely dominant, and one nearly dormant.

All occupations have an ideal profile of the senses, a need for one or two or three senses to be strong, and a particular preferred pattern of relationship between the three. Our success in our chosen walk of life is a function of the care with which we match our aptitudes to the profession we choose. Genetic patterns (like broad shoulders) can be significant factors in occupational choice, and it may be that our sensory patterns are, to an extent, genetically borne too. It is the relative levels of our ease in using each of the three primary senses, and the degree of ease with which we both learn and then use what we have learned, which are the parameters which we should test if we want to understand 'intelligence' and manage its development more effectively. As our sensory aptitudes are apparent at a fairly young age, and have great significance for our learning, perhaps there really is a case here for testing quite young children, so that their course through our educational system is directly focused on their individual needs and capacities.

Growing up

Flirting, our way of describing part of the process of trying out and finally selecting a life partner, is a culmination of the phase of behaviour which we begin when we enter puberty. Our first ten years are largely focused on the relationships we have with older people, establishing patterns which have considerable force in later life. At puberty, though, we become far more aware of our relationships with our peers, and those patterns of social contact and relative isolation which I have already described as characteristic of adult behaviour begin to emerge and settle.

One of the primary mechanisms by which our behaviour patterns (I am talking about behaviour now rather than the motivations which I have so far emphasised as of primary significance) are established is a sort of hybrid of copying and experimenting. We try out other people's behaviours to see whether they suit us.

The whole gamut of social and cultural influences weighs on this process of individualisation, in which the degree of differentiation we each aim to achieve for ourselves is a particular characteristic of our late twentieth century culture. At each stage, the experiments' success are confirmed or denied by a complex web of perceptions of our peers' opinions of the results, as well as those of our adults and ourselves. The relationship between these different sources of validation and approval is conditioned by, and conditions, the motivational patterns described above. Loners seek to confirm their sense of personal worth, so far as that's possible, by either sliding quietly into a safely anonymous conformity, or by taking on identities that protect their more vulnerable parts from probing enquiry. Clingies might also quietly hide within a group, avoiding being disliked, but active clingies will forge ahead at this stage, flying a flag to see how far they can get. Oblivious to the incompleteness of personality-security which renders them vulnerable to attack, active clingies will establish a bridgehead for the position they then they want to hold, blindly risking that displeasure of their peers which, as years go by, will inhibit such boldness for most of them. The clingy's sense of security comes from the so far unchallenged certainty of Mummy and Daddy's admiration for all they do; their problems come into focus now, as they discover that their friends are less forgiving of their arrogance and self-absorption.

All the copying and experimenting has some impact on our sense of relationship to society at large, but as we get a little older, the initial focus on relationships within groups narrows to a focus on relationships with other particular individuals. We acquire 'best friends' whose opinion of us is elevated to parent-like status, but subject to our own opinions: our 'best friend's' special function is to be a parent whose views we are permitted to refute.

For many young teenagers, it's usual to develop a strong sense of admiration for an adult they do not—cannot—know personally. Pop stars, tv heros and heroines, sports personalities: all these provide a pool from which we can choose an 'ideal stranger' to practice building a relationship with. Some, but by no means all, of us say that we have 'fallen in love' with our idols, and we seem to be remarkably blind to gender at this stage in our emotional development. The most important thing about the 'ideal stranger's' function for us is that we should be in absolute command of our relationship with them. That is not to say that we are (or feel) in command of our feelings for them: on the contrary, the whole point of these trial relationships is that we should be free to practice falling in and out of love, and falling in and out of a range of other emotions, with someone who is (we know for certain) unable to contradict us, or be in any way active in the relationship. Aunts and uncles will not do for this job (though they sometimes figure as the pattern develops), for the key to the pattern is the individual's certainty of being in control. No matter how complete the teenager's absorption may seem to them, or to outsiders, it is actually the certainty of these trial relationships' fictionality that makes it safe for them to be so absorbing, so apparently emotionally committed.

At widely different ages, but for most of us by twenty or so, we find that this training ground has come to feel sterile: the unreality of the idolising relationships has served its purpose, and we begin to focus on real relationships with real people. Our play-acting has given us (most of us) just enough confidence to have a crack at reality.

As with the experimental idolising, there's a complex pattern of gender mixing at this stage which I will not attempt to tackle here. Boys and girls who have already polarised into 'safe' same-sex groups at the first stage of puberty only gradually emerge as bold enough individuals to tackle their favoured-sex partners, and a wonderful variety of group contrivances exist and are invented to make this process of individual emergence easier, less fearsome.

In the end, though, each individual, if they are to form a bond with another, has to take the plunge and talk to and smile at someone they 'fancy'.

'Fancying', to take a temporary side-step from the main line of argument here, seems to depend on a pattern learned by the child from its mother at a very early stage. Melanie Klein's research of the 1940s has been supported by more recent studies, and has never conflicted with my own experience in working with people: it seems to be the case that we learn a model of an 'ideal outsider' from the things our mother communicates to us (I carefully avoid the oversimplification 'says') about our father. He becomes our model of the 'second-best', a template of the person from whom the nearest we might hope to get to our mother's 'warm unconditional regard' (Carl Rogers[10]) might be achieved. It seems clear that our mother's views are either expressed, or heard, in terms of the sensory patterns discussed earlier, because we always choose our partners applying tests of their suitability in reverse order of our sense patterns. Our schedule for choosing our partners will eliminate the quality we deal with least effectively first, and will tend to be most simplistic in its requirements. That is, if our order of senses goes visual best, feelings second and sound third, we would choose from a range of prospective partners who sounded similar to each other, and like our mother's view of our father's most admirable qualities in this respect. For some that might mean relative silence, and for others relative chattiness. Some are impressed by apparently 'intelligent' articulacy, and some by equally impressive quietitude. Once the risk or discomfort of unfamiliar challenges in our third sense has been eliminated, our second sense comes into play. Here we have greater room for variety, but still a compulsory exclusion of unfamiliarity or difficulty to some degree. Only with the final, first and best, sense are we free to choose at will, for in this respect alone can we cope with, and even enjoy, challenge.

One consequence of this pattern is interesting because it forces an admixture of sensory patterns between partners, which suggests an interesting structure of necessary variation if the sensory patterns are indeed genetically carried. Someone choosing a partner for their articulacy when, and because, they themselves are primarily visual, is going to be in partnership with someone they are likely to have difficulty in communicating with later on. Their children, whether these patterns are inherited or learned, will have the chance of either pattern for themselves, creating variety within the family unit as well as the potential for communication difficulties.

Another insight emerging from this application of the sensory scale is that arguments about the propriety of selecting partners on, say, looks alone, or any other single quality, are inherently incapable of resolution. All of us are bound to eliminate one sense first in a relatively crude way to exclude the risk of unfamiliarity. Equally, all of us then go on to a more complex execution of choice with our two remaining senses, so that it isn't really true that any of us do use 'looks' or any other quality literally alone.

One oddity of the way in which we learn our sexual template is that all of us, whatever our gender, are taught to admire the best qualities of our father as the best alternative to mother's own care. Although gender swapping takes place at puberty, it is the father's type, filtered through the mother's perception, which is encouraged to survive by the way the system works.

Let us return to the main line of argument: when we 'fancy' a partner, we have in the end to make an approach to them, or signal to them that we would like them to make an approach to us. This involves a hugely significant inversion of our 'normal' character (personality type), whose central forms have been forged or conditioned in the previous few years. Whether or not we are born clingy or loner, as I believe we are, the patterns are certainly conspicuous in our behaviour and motivation after the onset of puberty. Clingies, whose basic strategy for gaining validation (an adult's substitute for mother's 'warm unconditional regard') is to wear their perceived faults on their sleeve saying 'Please accept me even though I have these faults', have to seem passive—not to seek approval, but to wait for it to be offered. Loners must put aside *their* basic pattern of seeking approval: although they fear the consequences of overtly seeking contact, they need to establish an 'anchor' relationship with a clingy whose willingness to validate them by staying with them provides a sort of security that is unintrusive enough to seem acceptable.

A clingy woman, says her social role, should not approach her admired choice asking for acceptance, but should wait quietly for his approach, while the socially approved male, the loner, has to put aside his reluctance to form a long-term commitment, and claim a partner with pretended self-confidence.

In other words, what our approved role-type people have to do in flirting, or negotiating a relationship, is to pretend to take on the other's brain-side characteristics. A loner male must behave as though he has a clingy's self-confidence and commitment to the future, and the clingy woman must hide behind a pretended shield of loner-like diffidence, taking great care not to let her 'wedding bells' ring in earshot.

For the half of men who are clingies, this is their one high moment in life's trail: they are licensed to seek the approval of potential partners in a way that is entirely comfortable to them, and many of them do so with repulsive enthusiasm. These are the medallion men, the compulsive womanisers, men trapped in a moment of a full life's span when their disinhibition about their desires seems to have social licence. Their frustration in recognising, usually far too late, that they cannot carry on their whole life as bullish teenagers can be devastating, just as their behaviour towards the people whose approval they seek can be a blight. They ought to be comfortable in finding their 'natural' role demanded of them for once, but the 'overdrive' of unaccustomed social approval for their instinctive behavioural drives is actually deeply upsetting.

Loner women, by contrast, have a terrible time at this point in their lives. Society says that they have to pretend to enjoy being harassed by men puffed up with self-confidence, when actually they are themselves between the certainty that the last thing they want is a relationship with one of these men, and the fear that their own perceived weaknesses, indefinable but certainly present, makes them inappropriate partners for anyone anyway. They believe that even if they did accept a man, they would soon be rejected once their weaknesses were uncovered.

Of course, I am presenting these emotions in relatively extreme terms to characterise the patterns I believe underlie all our behaviour at this stage in our lives. As I shall explain later, there is strong evidence that only a small number of us suffer as badly as this, with readily recognisable, sad, consequences.

Essentially, then, I am saying that the experimenting with copying others which we begin as youngsters in dressing up games, and which we continue in early puberty in hero worship, individualisation and grouping behaviours, now finds its first significant use: in order to find an appropriate (like Mum's view of the best of Dad) partner, we have to 'swap sides', behaving like a clingy if we're a loner, and like a loner if we're a clingy. It's a part of the burden that this role stereotyping places on us that aberrant behaviour is inescapable for the clingy male and the loner woman, with the unpleasant consequences for both described above.

Falling in love

When we believe we've fallen in love—that is, found a good match to the template we learned from Mum—I believe that our copying comes to a natural high point. It seems to me that the aping of the opposite type's behaviour which we've followed so far now becomes a temporary reality, and the highly emotional bonding which takes place between young lovers actually involves temporarily living from the 'away' side instead of the 'home' side of our brains. We fall into reciprocal bonds with our new partners, feeling a security that allows clingies to feel independent, and loners to feel secure. The dizziness, the lack of concentration, the emotional commitment—all these are not the product of simply 'being in love' in a merely narrative way: they are a manifestation of our brain function's temporary inversion. In a real sense, being in love makes each of us complete, gives us an experience of being other, which sets up (ideally) a capacity for empathy and coherence as adults. Being in love is necessarily, therefore, a joining of a clingy and a loner.

I believe that what is meant to happen as this inversion fades, and we gradually return to our 'home' sides, is that we should remain bonded to this first partner, confident of their securing and validating love, and able, through the security gained from empathetic exchange and shared experience, to develop our own particular strengths more vigorously than before. Our partnership now contains a 'plugged-in' resource of 'other-ness'. What happens too often in societies—not just ours—is that social expectations of various kinds defeat the optimal function of this pattern for many couples, and individuals are either trapped in inappropriate relationships on the whim of outsiders, perhaps for the sake of a property deal or a business contract, or their social aspirations or ludicrous emotional ambitions (one might say malfunctions) encourage them to reject a loved partner for one they suppose might bring social success, or more 'love'. One of the great flaws in our handling of relationships (which these attempts at understanding are meant to help resolve) is that we harbour a fantasy, encouraged by our image-makers, that we can live in a perpetual state of renewing love: that the excitement and intensity of this first empathetic exchange is a model of how a relationship ought to feel all the time, and so that if it changes (matures), it is failing. Our pathetic attempts to 'stay young' by trading in partners, hoping that the thrill of newness will last next time we try, are, if my model of what is really happening is correct, hopelessly doomed.

If I'm right, then it must be true that adult relationships are meant to depend on remembered bonding, rather than on the continual rebonding which our society prizes. Copulation for fun for life—perpetual puberty—is, in my terms, at odds with the physiological psychology I'm advancing. Once we've met our match, loners need to find other kinds of excitement to fill their present than relationship-swapping (job development and child-rearing are the traditional challenges to boredom), and clingies have to accept that winning notches on their stick is a pathetic and only temporarily functional validation-substitute.

The male midlife crisis and anorexia

If you're a loner man, the congruence between the way you feel and the way society expects you to behave is pretty good, so you don't have too many problems (except, as I've explained, with flirting and forming relationships). Equally, if you're a clingy woman, things are relatively straightforward, because the things you want for yourself (a family, security and so on) are the things society wants to see you cherishing.

As we've seen, if you're a clingy man, you have more difficulty trying to conform to patterns you don't like. But there are some points in your life where unaccustomed congruence allows release: flirting is a licence to ask to be loved, so some get stuck in that phase. More significantly, the drive which makes all of us aim to reclaim the security of our mother's 'warm unconditional regard' (something which unhappy loners cannot believe was genuine—see R.D.Laing's *Divided Self*[9] for a description of the loner personality *in extremis*), generates a real problem for clingy men who have to cope with their family's changing emotional demands on them.Clingy men will always be aware of the conditionality of their partner's regard for them: their loners will have needed to preserve enough independence to feel 'safe' in themselves, and not so drawn into their clingy's world that they feel absorbed, suffocated, identity-less. When this pair of clingy and loner, at ease to some degree with the strengths of the balance they've achieved between each other's needs, have children, there's a tendency for the clingy Dad to ease into an absolutely relaxed enjoyment of his children's authentically unconditional regard. Though his wife may think a great deal of him, there will always be some slight consciousness of reserve. This limitation vanishes in the parent-child relationship, where the adult's protective power is greatly valued by both. When the children grow to puberty, they seek independence from this power, needing to establish themselves as adults in their own right. Whatever the sex of the child, the clingy Dad loses his prop, and if (in the course of concentration on rearing children) his relationship with his wife has been allowed to 'go on hold', he may be left with less emotional support than he needs—and a lot less than he's been used to while the children have been growing up. If the child is a daughter, the withdrawal from this close relationship can be traumatic for her, too. In my experience (I put it no stronger, so that 'scientists' may go and check with their own 'data') manic-depression amongst men in their forties (of which I have seen many instances) is frequently associated with (I hesitate to suggest 'triggered', though that's what I really mean) the withdrawal from dad's emotional support of a pubescent child. If, I'm arguing, you have a clingy dad, a weakened relationship with a loner woman who's been keen to develop her own independent identity, and a withdrawing child (perhaps more dangerously, a withdrawing daughter), then what you have is a man at risk of manic-depression or a stressed malfunction of his clingy personality which is a step or two towards that extreme.

If you have a clingy Dad, perhaps with a compromised relationship with loner Mum but not always, and a pubescent *loner* daughter, then it may be the daughter that's at risk. Her experience of growing up has been (to the extent that it's been self-conscious) one of seeking to explain to herself why she feels bad about herself, not sure of who she is, and at risk of obliteration by emotionally dominant outsiders. She projects a sexual interpretation of her childhood backwards onto originally innocent experiences (that is, experiences with no immediate sexual content or connotation: I cannot attempt to explain the problems which actual abuse imposes on its victims), sometimes believing that she has actually been abused (when she hasn't), and always feeling guilty about her relationship with her parents. What we have is the 'Electra' complex acting at its most potent: the girl elicits a fond smile from her Dad as a baby, which at the time she reads as a signal of her special power over him, as a winning of his affection for her in preference to her mother; read back sexually later, the girl feels guilty about having 'taken' her father's loyalty from her mother (remember we're talking about a family where there's a clingy Dad and a loner Mum, so this reading of her own experience is going to be reinforced by the realities of the parent's relationship, even if the reasons for these relations being as they are are beyond the child's understanding). As the girl reaches puberty, the guilt about her mother's stolen partner generates a complex and deeply ambivalent relationship with Mum, desperate for affirmation and forgiveness—and a much less complex but far more emotionally heightened relationship with Dad, almost always a violent rejection of him struck through with a desperation to reclaim the 'innocent' protection remembered from pre-conscious childhood. In these circumstances, one of the strategies a loner girl can adopt to protect herself from what she reads as the terrible potential consequences of growing to adulthood is not to eat, or to eat and then vomit. These, in my experience, are the circumstances in which anorexia, bulimia for young women and manic-depression for middle-aged men (their 'mid-life crisis') emerge. If my observations are right (and they are based on twenty years of work with many individuals), then families 'at risk' are very easily recognisable, and these problems should be ones we can step in early to prevent, or at least control.

Being gay

Being gay, which I believe is the consequence of one of our genetic bipolar switches being 'thrown' in the 'other' direction, so that its on-off status interacts with a cluster whose impact includes some predication of the degree of sexual urgency an individual feels, causes a similar kind of conflict with social models.

If a loner man is gay, his socially comfortable personality is compromised by his 'unmasculine' desire to have sex and relationships with other men. Only if such sexual relations are of great importance to him will he break through social taboos and 'come out' as gay.

On the other hand, a clingy man who is gay has a reason for feeling as he does about relationships: the pattern society calls 'feminine', wanting to be loved and to have security for the future (by social convention with a strong independent man) fits the gay clingy man even better than it fits the clingy woman. No wonder, then, that our society's dominant gay stereotype is of a limp-wristed effeminate man, a sort of pathetic imitation of a woman.

Society's model of a 'loner' masculine ideal is compounded for clingy gay men because the number of actual loner men they are given the right to address is diminished by the latter's reluctance to 'come out'. A loner will always be reluctant to allow their 'faults' to be seen; being gay, while society continues to call it a fault, is a good reason for staying as quiet as possible.

There's therefore a numerical imbalance of 'out' clingy gay men to loners that's a reflection of the pressure of social taboos on the individual. The clingy's enjoyment of being emotionally validated by being the subject of attention, having their faults discussed rather than having their virtues praised, encourages the stereotype and variants of it to persist, and enforces social prominence for it.

Lesbians have an identical problem, turned the other way around. The dominant public image of a 'butch' lesbian has emerged because it's the independent loner who has been forced to strike out from the stereotypical life a woman has been meant to lead. A clingy lesbian can, says society, survive by 'thinking of England', but a loner lesbian will resist the overwhelming power of a man's dominance in sex if it's not what she wants. Good sex, it should be said, is about exchanging power—both partners must necessarily be self-absorbed at the moment of climax even if everything else about the sexual act is conditioned by the wish to please the partner—and if one partner is perceived by their partner as taking power, while the other only loses it, then the sex is bad. It's not just lesbians who have this problem: a lack of confidence about their right to take power in sex has compromised many women's (and some men's) experience of it. Given Foucault's proposition that our culture characteristically talks about sex instead of doing it, we can see some of this problem, the rights to take power and to give it, expressed tangentially in current discussion of sexual power in cases of rape and sexual abuse.

Gay people wish to be equal, to be treated just like any other ordinary members of the community. If the stereotypical roles we force on youngsters were released so that we could be who we are, not who we are meant to be, this could be achieved.

The dominance of feeling

A paradox that I cannot explain, but have to address, is the way all of us, whether loner or clingy, find that our most precious emotional and intellectual experiences are right-brain ones, not left. The quality of self-absorption and immersion in our experience is one we cherish, whether sexual (as described above) or musical, theatrical or political, loving or charitable. The climax of feeling we call 'the best' is an expression of the right-brain taking over, the left brain trusting it not to lose control.

Exactly this model of trust operates in hypnosis: the rationality of the left-brain is temporarily suspended, and we accept 'suggestions' because they feel good (or in the case of curses' and hexes' hypnotic function, because they feel appropriately bad). I don't understand (yet) exactly what happens in extreme elation, and in the hypnosis we have learned to use to exploit its effect. I suspect that the 'valve' function I described earlier goes into some sort of override, hormonally pumped in a way that allows it to feel absent, lifted: but I don't know—I am only wondering. Perhaps you may understand better.

The importance of empathy

Our society enjoys self-absorption, both in its community life as patriotism and insularity, and in our lives as individuals. The justification for selfish behaviour, that it promotes social wellbeing by the achievement of personal strength in the eventual interest of us all, originated in the philosophies of the mid-seventeenth century, when economic conditions made personal survival urgent and significant in a way that they do not today. There are two things that make self-absorption feel good in the Cartesian sense. Self-absorption guarantees being right (or seems to)—we must (we think) know what is best for us, when we take no account of anyone else. Secondly, trying to consider other people's attitudes and feelings is far more complicated and prone to error than simply relying on feeling and doing it 'your way'. The problem, though, as I've shown throughout this book, is that although there's some philosophical truth in the perception that we are inescapably separate from each other, having real difficulty in 'knowing' each other's thoughts, we are no worse off in understanding each other's thoughts than we are in understanding the 'real' world we've tried to objectify over the last three hundred years. The notions of relativity which have destabilised our understanding of scientific 'facts' in the past hundred years also expose the inadequacy of sceptical isolation as a model for functional thinking: everything we think about is as relative as everything else; subjectivity does not exist, because there is no objectivity with which to contrast it. Although we can withdraw to our inner consciousness, we cannot be any more certain of emotional 'realities' than concrete ones, and the other way around too.

As a description of a philosophical position, an account of the recent passage of philosophical understanding of our place in the world, what I've just said is reasonably standard: it expresses pretty much the position any philosopher might take now about 'the human condition'.

What I want to observe, without being able to explain, is that the old model of our place in the world (the selfish one) is pretty close to a clingy's (right-brained) world view, and although I've suggested that its roots lie in seventeenth century philosophy, it's been the nineteenth and twentieth centuries whose culture it has dominated. It's not just the self-absorption that signals a connection to right-brain activity: it's also characteristic of this outlook that it believes in planning towards a better future, controlling the present for future gain, and always in terms of the past.

The 'new' outlook is just as clearly left-brain in its form: the timescale backwards and forwards has gone, and the scale of differentiation is between inner awareness and external action. Selfishness is allowable for survival's sake, and we are nervous about our status in relation to others whose attitude to us we feel insecure about. We cope by releasing the future from our thoughts, retreating into parochialism and little committees capable of direct personal control. Global schemes, the dreams of our twentieth century megalomaniacs for universal power, are rejected, and we have little grey men instead, whose job it is to try not to make too many mistakes. The eighteenth century's optimistic rationalism has something in common with our attitude now: we buffer ourselves from a fear of the unknowable (the spiritual so beloved of the Romantics) by believing that one day everything will be alright, if only we make sure that the detail in front of our nose is tackled properly.

I don't understand why our culture swings in its phases between left and right-brain models, either in the way we think about ourselves, or in the way we admire particular character traits at different times. Try working out the brain-side dominance of culturally significant figures over the past three hundred years: it's really difficult to tell about eighteenth century and very recent figures, usually a good sign of left-brain dominance (remember that they resist 'being known' out of a dread of suffocation or absorption), while the strong dominance of right-brain 'look at me and my faults' characters from the late eighteenth to the late twentieth century is all too obvious, especially when you recognise the particular clingy trait of *daring* anyone to challenge the status that's claimed. Our power-crazed leaders have all seemed ripe for a fall to outsiders, but managed not to fall for such a very long time within their own cultures. Look at the difficulty we have in appreciating the true objectives of an artist like Mozart, struggling to be expressive in a Romantic way (virtually inventing the idea that audience members should 'identify' with the experience of a character on stage, feeling the character's experience as though it were their own in Tamino's role in *The Magic Flute*) when he has himself a left-brain personality. See how easily a right-brain personality like Haydn emerges from an uncomfortable youth with the 'wrong' personality for the temper of his age to a glorious Indian summer, with no crude change of style needed, but an *almost* invisible relaxation into complete emotional empathy in his last works, which may now legitimately speak from the heart as well as the mind. Joseph Wright of Derby, similarly, emerges from a contrived self-consciousness in his early works towards a relaxed ease in his last—unfortunately, though, with the consequence that the quality of many of his late works is weak and uncontrolled, where the vigour and inventiveness of his early pieces allow feeling to thrive as a gloss on their narrative content. Advertisements for the sale of his services ('Look—I can paint your family better than anyone else, and I'm damned clever with light effects too') are hung on clever ideas for subjects which allow the portrait sampler and the demonstration of technique to cohere *and* assert the brilliance of the artist.

The doctrine of this book is a product of its time: instead of preaching the virtues of self-absorption, the excellence of extremity, it seeks to achieve balance in the belief that evenhandedness between people as individuals and in social groups is best. If we 'empathise' with other people, that is, seek to understand their motivations and objectives, so that they can be helped to achieve their aims in a way that doesn't conflict with others' needs, but is to the general good, I believe that all of us will be better off. Personal empathy and social empathy seem to me to be the best basis for a culture's security and strength. That I should feel this is only a measure of my place in time: I am, quite clearly, of my culture in late twentieth century Britain. How far what I have had to say may be seen to be value or insight in the future is less important than its usefulness now—a very eighteenth century outlook.

Power

Where Freud, in the last years of the nineteenth century and the first of the twentieth, saw sex as the focus of the force that 'drives' our personalities, we now see 'power' taking that same dominant role. 'Translating' Freud, writing 'power' for 'sex', has an extraordinary (if you haven't thought about it) modernising impact, bringing what he says to contemporary relevance, even if it doesn't resolve the peculiarities and difficulties of a good deal of what he had to say.

But is it true that power really is the force that drives us, any more than sex was before? The truth of either depends on a model of human motivation which has an instinctive force conditioning desire (the survival instinct, posited by Darwin, neatly encompasses both sex and power), so that present activity is always the product of our awareness of its future value. As I've explained, this model of mental activity is a good description of a 'clingy's' outlook—just as Freud's perception of his work was hugely and obviously conditioned by his assumption that his own personality was essentially identical in its forms and pattern to everyone else's (where I am offering a two-type model instead). Because it depends on the clingy perception of time, the *idea* that sex or power dominates our consciousness is itself a 'right-brain' idea. Its acceptance over the past hundred years or more, and the increasing reluctance we feel in accepting the idea's truth, is evidence of cultural phasing (the temporary dominance in a culture's development of one personality type and then the other). We need a different way of understanding human interaction—a loner one—that will bring us a new sense of what psychology is, and how it might work, for the left-brain dominated age we are entering.

Let's say that our 'drive' (what I've been calling our motivation), whether you think it is based on power, sex or survival, acts in a balancing pattern between personalities. The clingy half of us are 'lateral' (past through the present towards the future) and the loner half are 'in-out' (introspection and exhilaration co-existing in degrees of depth of present experience, with the 'absent' self being part of the 'present' social creature). This model doesn't present a simplistic pattern of 'I want power over you' against 'I want to stop you having power over me', but is more complex, in a way that seems to square better with our modern perception of the complexity of personality and its motivations.

The practical part: what to do about it

What we've got is a model of the human mind that has two main elements: that our motivations for action depend on whether we are either left- or right-brain hemisphere dominated (we are one or the other—there's no 'bit of both' in *this* part of the scheme); and that our ways of communication (learning and then using what we've learned) are conditioned by a 'wiring diagram' that puts our three main senses in an explicit order of priority. Although we've talked in the earlier part of this book about other conditioning factors, and about the signs that nature and nurture are both involved in these patterns, what we're going to do now is try to set up a practical guide to using the system. This section of the book can't provide a complete guide to every strategy, or solve every problem: it aims, though, to give a few suggestions that indicate a strategy for problem-solving. Think about the sheer variety of personalities inherent in the model I've proposed: two basic motivational types, clingy and loner, and two sets of character pairs, active–passive and positive–negative, then individual 'orders of senses' that condition our learning and communication processes. That's a huge number of different possible personality 'types', even before you consider the impact of our social and educational experience on us. Even with all this variety, though, understanding our motivations, *why* we make our choices, helps a great deal. So, if the observations at the heart of the analysis are right, then trying to do more of the things that are 'natural' for us in a way that reinforces and exploits, rather than contradicts, our brain-side dominance, and being more honest about why we do things so that we make real choices, not pretend ones, should make all of us happier.

Working out which type you are: (clingies and loners first...)

The only barrier to understanding which type we are ourself is the fact that all of us are trained to try and conform to a stereotype that fits some of us quite well some of the time, and some of us very badly some of the time. Everyone has a time when the stereotype isn't such a bad fit as usual, and that's a great help in spotting what's really going on.

There are two sets of pattern recognition to do, so to make life easier, let's tackle them one at a time: brain hemisphere dominance (whether you're a 'clingy' or a 'loner') first.

Basically, a clingy (someone whose brain's right hemisphere is dominant) is pretty much the stereotype of what a woman's meant to be like, and a loner (someone whose brain's left hemisphere is dominant) is what our society says a man should be like.

Although the labels I'm using are pretty crude, they do characterise one feature of each type's behaviour under stress: when a clingy is miserable, they'd like someone to make them a cup of tea, or cheer them up, or sit with them: getting less miserable depends on someone else 'validating' you, making you feel better by being there. A miserable loner wants the exact opposite: they need to get away from other people when they're miserable, so that they can pull themselves together out of sight. They find other people's offers of support invasive, and the last thing they want is to be made a cup of tea, or to have their hand held.

Why that is, I've discussed in earlier chapters, which also have a less crude description of the character types. Some of that might be helpful later in confirming your first identification of which type you think you are.

Remember that because society says men should be loners and women should be clingies, there's a fair chance that if you're a clingy man (and half the men are clingy) your 'I want someone to be nice to me' behaviour might be a bit squashed. If you're a loner woman, unless you've had a fairly stormy teenage, you might well value quite a lot of the things that relationships and children have to offer—but you should still be able to recognise the sensation of relief you feel when you have a few minutes to yourself. If you are lucky and you've got the personality structure that's official for your gender, it's quite likely that your 'be nice to me' or 'leave me alone' behaviour will be built into your daily routine, and won't seem particularly significant. A loner man might find independence in having to get on with work on his own, or just getting the beers in for his mates at the pub, while a clingy woman might get the company she needs from belonging to the WI, or occasional visits to friends.

Another way of telling which personality structure you have (which ought to help, but which some people find confusing) is to work out which brain-side is your partner's dominant one, and then assume that yours is the other—a good relationship is normally between one of each. The reason it's confusing is precisely the reason we're not as happy as we could be: our behaviour is averaged towards a 'norm' so that we don't seem too selfish to others, and because to some extent all of us roll into the middle of the personality mattress when we're relatively calm—being able to relax towards the average is part of a sensible definition of happy! (See 'Behavioural convergence: Getting it together' earlier in the book for a discussion of why averaging is such an important part of being happier.) Still, if you look honestly enough at *why* you make your choices, and why you think your partner makes theirs (perhaps thinking about other partners you've had too—the 'nearly alright' ones will be opposite personality types to you, and the 'complete dead loss' ones will be the same as you) you should be able to learn to tell who's what.

If you're the loner, you'll go out with friends to enjoy the occasion, for 'now', and be reluctant to spend all the time out planning the next trip or reminiscing about the last. You don't mind planning things for the future, but can't understand why other people (clingies) get so worked up about changing the plans and doing something else instead. You'll dislike *always* having to do anything, and especially you'll dislike always having to take your partner with you when you go out. Being able to spread yourself around different groups, probably groups who don't know each other, and who you would prefer to keep separate, is important. On the whole you don't like 'friends' knowing your personal business, and when you do need advice from a friend (say a lawyer or a builder you know at the pub) you're quite likely to talk to them about your problem as though it's an abstract one—not out of embarrassment at your own difficulty, but just because you don't like people knowing your business. Having one of your friends turn up on your doorstep unannounced is one of the most annoying things that can happen to you.

If you're the clingy, going out with friends will be really important to you, but you'd probably rather have them come to see you at home, and giving them a meal or having them stay will be a real treat. In fact there's a good chance that you've chosen where you live so that there's room to entertain visitors. A friend turning up unannounced is great (as long as you haven't got things to do that someone else more important will praise you for having finished or blame you for not having finished!) and you probably drop hints to people that you quite like being visited, or phoned up with invitations to go and see them. You have lots of material possessions that you don't like throwing away when they're past usefulness, because of the associations they represent—only the rarest clingies don't have a favourite mug for tea, which their tame loner usually has a special knack of breaking—and some of which at least are chosen to impress other people rather than because you particularly want them. When you're miserable, you'll be cheered up by someone offering a treat in the future: 'let's go out shopping together the week after next' is enough to clear substantial misery, and a failure to keep this promise can be submerged if another, almost identical and probably just as unreliable, is forthcoming. You have a routine, like things staying the same, and although you like meeting new people and adding them to your list of people who like you, you particularly like keeping friends for a long time, and are disappointed when they move away, or lose interest in you. You're a bit of a mixer, and quite like putting friends of yours who don't know each other together to see how they get on—and probably get into trouble for trying to get your (loner) partner's friends to mix with yours and (even worse) to become your friends too, when what your loner wants and needs are independent friendships to which they can escape when you're too clingy to bear. You're a dreadful blabbermouth, always telling people your problems and innermost thoughts, even when you know that your partner's going to be furious that shared private information has been published. Because you look forwards to things that have been planned, you get frustrated by the way other people (loners) never seem to have the same sense of a plan being definite as you do, and that they don't seem to mind (or care) if things are cancelled or altered.

Of course, this kind of anecdotal description is securely based on the lives of nice middle class professionals, and if that's not who you are, the fit might not be all that good. I hope it's just good enough at characterising the *motivations* of the two personality types for you to spot yourself, and have a pretty clear idea that your partner (or the people you fancy) are the other type.

Working out which type *they* are

We get on best with people who are the opposite type to ourselves, especially where there's the prospect of a sexual or emotional partnership forming. Someone who's almost exactly like us (a brother or sister, or a friend at school or work) might be *really* annoying; we seem to hate people who are the same type as us and have nearly—but not quite—the same behaviour. Sometimes there's an obvious clue—they might have dreadful table manners, or pick their nose, when you go to great lengths to avoid both—but if you think about it (or ask someone else) you'll find that you're very much like the people you hate.[11] If there's someone in your life you really can't stand, there's a good chance they're just like you!

In a way, the most important judgment to get right is the one we've used our instincts to manage for centuries: choosing a partner. Although some brother-

and-sister-like relationships do work, especially in gay communities where 'sex for fun' with outsiders is socially acceptable to some degree, in general a sexual and emotional relationship between two adults only has tightness and energy when it includes complementary personalities, one of each type.

That means that you can learn to spot other people of the opposite type to yourself by learning to recognise the special qualities of the people you fancy, and then recognising the presence of those qualities in others whom you don't actually fancy (perhaps because they're the wrong sex) but who have the same 'buzz' about them.

Because all of us have to deal with other people at home and at work, it's really constructive to be able to tell whether they're 'clingy' or 'loner', because then you can get the best out of them. I have to say, too, for completeness' sake, that knowing what someone really wants or doesn't want gives you a great deal of power over them!

Recognising the eye patterns

When you ask someone a question—or when someone asks you a question—what happens inside your head is reflected in the way your eyes behave. If you're thinking in images (visually), when you stop looking at the other person directly, your eyes go upwards; if you're thinking in sounds (aurally) they go sideways;

and if you're thinking in feelings (kinæsthetically) they go downwards. All of these directional changes go to one side or the other: your eyes go to the side of your strongest hand (the one you write, or chose to do most jobs with) if you're remembering, and they go to the side of your weaker hand if you're imagining.

So someone right-handed remembering visually to answer a question would, when they pull away from eye contact with you to think, find their eyes had gone up and to their right. If they were thinking aurally, their eyes would go straight to the right when remembering, and straight to the left when imagining. Thinking in feelings shows as a downward movement, right or left depending on whether the person is remembering or imagining. Left-handed people do just the same, but their eyes go to the left when they're remembering, and to the right when they're imagining. Although you would, perhaps, expect there to be some correlation between right- and left-handedness and what I've been describing as right- and left-brain hemisphere dominance, it doesn't seem to be very strong: only a slight prevalence of left-handedness amongst 'creative' people like architects, who need to be good at using the right-hand side of their brains to deal with spatial constructs, suggests any link at all, and architects come with either side of their brain dominant in personality terms, regardless of their right- or left-handedness, as far as I can tell.

The only eye pattern that can be a little difficult to read is the visual; it's the commonest one, and although some people's eyes do a nice clear upwards movement, a lot of people thinking visually have eyes that only lift a little way over the horizon, as though they're just looking over your shoulder while they think about the question you've asked them. Because thinking visually seems to be the commonest pattern, and thinking aurally the least common, if you're in doubt about a movement that looks more sideways than up, you're more likely to be right if you read it as remembering or imagining visually than aurally.

The other positions are usually pretty clear, and don't leave much room for misinterpretation.

All of us have got one sense that we normally use first most of the time. Our eyes go to that position first and stay there longest. They flick to a second position, usually just briefly, immediately before we answer the question we've been thinking about. This is the secondary, or check sense, and again, most of us usually use the same one most of the time. The third sense is the one we use least easily, and our eyes only rarely go to its position. If you're asked a question someone else might expect you to use this particular sense to think about, you'll normally 'translate' the question so that your 'first' sense can deal with it for you. For example, if your eyes don't go down very often, and 'feeling' is your third sense, if someone asks you what your breakfast tasted like, you'd probably (depending on which of the other two senses you normally used first) either think of what someone else's face looked like while they ate it, or remember what someone had said about the taste at the time. This isn't because we can't use our third senses at all: just that we much prefer using the first, and if necessary the second.

Because your sense-order has a huge impact on your learning strategies and experience of every aspect of your life, it also has a huge importance in understanding your preferences and means of expression. It is, too, of central significance as you choose and develop career paths and hobbies. Recognising someone's sense-order gives you a tremendously illuminating insight into their lives, because the way they build their 'knowledge bank' and then use it will be entirely subject to their sensory strategies.

Dealing with people like you

This isn't as easy as it sounds, not just because the clash of personalities that are too close for comfort makes us reluctant to recognise some likenesses, but because something we all do because we don't stop to think about it—assume that everyone else thinks exactly as we do until reality proves our assumption untenable—makes it more difficult to recognise and cope with the small differences between basically like personalities than the real contrasts between clingies and loners.

It's when you're trying to *use* the patterns we've been studying that the two additional sets I introduced at the outset, but haven't discussed since, come into their own. Although motivated by the same basic urges, a relatively passive person, whether clingy or loner, will be vastly different in their behaviour to a relatively active person with the same personality structure. A person whose strategies for achieving their ends are, on the whole, positive (being nice to get people to like them, for example) will seem hugely different to someone who protects themself from rejection by being really nasty to everyone. By being deliberately negative, these people know they're keeping control of their relationships. Their basic motivation, to control other people's regard for them so that at least the important people's opinions are positive, is the same as that of the *positive* character's. Although someone who uses negativity in this way might not necessarily feel negative inside, their insecurities about their likeability, with the behaviour they have copied from their families as children, mean that they feel safer hiding behind an unpleasant shell, telling themselves that someone who really cares about them would see through it and come close anyway.

Nonetheless, the obvious is true: if someone seems to you to have the same basic outlook as your own, even if their ordinary behaviour seems fairly different, you're likely to get on well with them if you assume that they like things you like, and think the way you do. So, to pick a single illustration of how this works in practice, if a clingy meets a clingy and they plan sharing a party for their friends, or organise some other event that will draw people to admire their skills, they're quite likely to get on well. Both will like having company, though both will probably prefer a loner's company to each other's. Two loners will get on well together if they forget about the future and have fun in the present, giving each other room as a relief from the pressure both feel from their clingies. Where clingies will nearly always ask loners to tell them how they feel, loners can feel safer with each other, away from such invasive irritants.

Dealing with people like them

Because 'they' are like the partners you have or would like, knowing how to deal with 'them' effectively is enormously important. The key to doing it successfully is to understand the basic contrast between the two personality structures we've identified. Where the clingy lives in perpetual awareness of the past and the future, and has a strong sense of what their personality is and what's wrong with it, the loner is focused on life now, and thinks not in terms of lateral time but (at a sort of 90° 3D tangent) in and out, standing with a sense of vacuum behind them, and potential experience in front. They know that they're supposed to have a defined sense of what their personality is, but they don't, and quite often feel that they ought to try and find one. They can't recognise that their characteristic energy, their commitment to the present, feels like a personality to other people, because they know that they change they way they behave quite considerably in different situations, whereas clingies stay the same wherever they are and whoever they're with. If you were going to try and oversimplify this contrast for the sake of clarity, you might say that the clingy was 'along' and the loner was 'in and out'. If you wanted to get pretty serious about understanding this contrast, you could look at the two kinds of mental activity described by the philosopher Martin Heidegger. He contrasts the kind of active thinking philosophers do (as well as ordinary people), where they're aware of what they're thinking about, and what they're thinking about it (which is left-brain activity), and what he calls 'coping-with' thinking, like chopping an onion while you think about something else or nothing, or hammering in a nail once you've got its basic position set (which is a right-brain activity). Heidegger's characterisations, 'active' and 'coping with', are misleading for our purposes, because all of us do both kinds of thinking, without one being 'better' than the other: we're greatly extending what we think the right-brain is in charge of. To be fair, only Kierkegaard and Nietsche had taken any professional notice of the fact that 'rational' thinking wasn't the only kind of mental activity we have before Heidegger tackled the issue.[12]

To deal with 'them' effectively, you have to try and understand the consequences of their different attitude to time, relationships and self. Loners will always worry about who exactly they are, and they're not likely to thank a clingy for inviting themselves into unwanted intimacy which makes their own sense of inner vacuum even worse. Equally, a clingy's not likely to think much of a loner who can't say out loud, 'I like you the way you are, with all these faults that matter more to you than to me; I really do love you.' If the loner has to bite their tongue at that point to stop themselves going on to say, 'but I really can't say whether I'll feel the same way tomorrow, let alone next week or next year', then so be it. The clingy has just as hard a time remembering not to let their wedding plans come out loud on a second (or even sometimes a first) date! Within the bounds of reasonable honesty (a word and a practice most of us only use as a weapon to hurt people), you'll get more out of 'them' if you give them more of what they want, and manage to be reasonably honest about what you want where that isn't in complete conflict with their needs. You can trade a night out on your own for a commitment to a day out with friends you don't like that much, but babies are too solid, and too demanding, to be anything except wanted by both partners in a relationship.

Getting the best out of them

If you've recognised their basic personality type—clingy or loner—and you're aiming for the greatest degree of congruence you can—being what they need you to be, helping them to get what they want out of you—the next step is to aim higher.

This is where your ability to recognise, and work with, the eye patterns becomes really useful. If the person you're with has vision as their strongest sense, you're going to communicate most effectively with them if you show them things rather than saying them. A left-out shopping list will have more chance of execution than a spoken reminder to buy toilet rolls, no matter how urgent the spoken request. Exactly the opposite applies if the person you're with is aural rather than visual: they will remember the speech, and not notice the written list unless you've told them it's there and what's on it. A kinæsthetic (feelings first) person will need to use a secondary sense to deal with shopping lists, and will only buy the things you want if you've asked them nicely, or if they've written the list out themselves.

We make amazing projections about 'good behaviour' onto other people because we assume that their mental apparatus must work like ours. If we find ourselves distracted by the tv, even if we're not interested by the programme on it, we assume that that's true for everyone. In fact it's characteristic of people with vision as their first sense that they can't help being dominated by things seen, and therefore that they are resistant to visual stimuli they can't control. A moving image will always take priority for a visual person. Equally, it's sound that dominates the world of aural people, who happily leave a tv on in a corner of a room while they read, but can't bear to have a radio on, or a record, because they can't help listening to it and being distracted from what they're meant to be doing. They can't understand how some people (the visual ones) can work (that is, read) when there's a record playing, because their way of reading is to convert the visual information into sound (reading out loud to themselves) and the 'real' sound easily dominates the 'translation'. This book has been written by someone for whom sound is the first sense: he thinks it shows, and that the grammar and syntax probably makes clearer sense read out loud than read visually. He knows that all the brackets and hyphenated phrases which he uses to suggest tone of voice probably infuriate visual readers, who prefer something that looks cleaner. He suspects that the book needs translating back into sound—by being 'read out loud—to make best sense. Kinæsthetic (feelings first) people are affected by a different set of distractions (if they're a loner, having people around, or if they're a clingy, not), and they're surprised by other people's ability to ignore the things they find difficult.

As you can see, this network of possibilities can build up into a pretty formidable matrix of dos and don'ts—and we've so far only looked at mostly positive qualities. If vision is your strongest sense, that doesn't necessarily mean that you like looking at things: it only means that you're very sensitive to what you see. Some 'visual' people find their sensitivity is hugely handicapping, because they can't bear untidiness, or the unusual. There are some colours that really make them cringe, and some kinds of visual environment that have a dramatic (and not necessarily very nice) impact on the way they feel. Equally, primarily aural people don't always like music and talking: they might find sound deeply disturbing and difficult, keeping away from loud noise, and dreading rooms full of people chatting. These are the people who turn on the radio for a particular programme and then turn it off, not being able to bear the continuity announcer's banter, or being forced to listen to music or talk they don't like. Perhaps I've been unlucky, but I've met more kinæsthetic people with difficulties arising from this kind of sensory inversion than the other two put together: vegans who don't like food have the same eye pattern as gourmets who can't stop eating; people who wear nasty plastic shoes or awful clothes because they don't care about such things, or worse, say they need to look dreadful because they care about the environment (as if caring about trees meant that you have to look like one)—these are the same, in pattern, as the glamour kittens in cashmere and fur, forever sensitive to the touch of their clothes on their skin.

In each case, every parameter I've described (brain-side, sensory patterns of priority) can be active or passive in its function, positive or negative in quality. How exactly people use their primary material and experiences life through their primary sense will be entirely coloured by which of the other two is secondary, and how the arrangement of active to passive and positive to negative operates on that, and therefore indirectly on the principal functions of the main sense. Add a third layer of the least easy sense, accept that because it's most difficult to use it's also most likely to throw up negatives and passives, and you begin to see how easy it is for each of us to feel entirely individual—and how easy it has been for the pattern I've described in this book (which has seemed so obvious to me for such a long time) has remained virtually hidden for so long. That it has emerged for me deserves, I think, the briefest of explanations: I think I have seen the pattern only because my own motivation has been to avoid rejection by seeming useful; in my determination to seem useful I have tried to learn how to quickly recognise the most important elements of what people want from me; in simplifying those observations (for example, whether to ape a doctor in white-coated formality for a loner, or to be cuddly and approachable for a clingy), the present work has developed.

Getting the best out of yourself

Although being happier depends enormously (and perhaps mainly) on being able to make other people happier, it seems only sensible to take responsibility for sorting out our own lives too. In the end, you're probably going to be the person who's most likely to understand your own motivation best, even if it's easier to work out your feelings by talking things through with a friend or neutral advisor—though remember that that's an aural person's point of view: if you're visual or kinæsthetic, you find your *own* equivalent!

Conclusion: Being happier...

There isn't a 'best' way to be, and the richness of our culture depends on the variety of its people's many interests and attitudes. But all of us can be happier if we make informed and careful decisions about our lives, instead of being bundled by other people and circumstances into situations and relationships that make us miserable.

Unfortunately for the loners, it's just not possible to exist in a state of perpetual happiness and excitement: there has to be some sort of down side for us to be able to tell that the good bits are special. Unfortunately for the clingies, you don't get a past to be nostalgic about, or a future to plan, unless you're prepared to engage with the present, to be an active participant in life as it comes. Although I've spent the whole of this book talking about personality as a biologically conditioned phenomenon, it's still up to us, what we make of our relationships. The recognition that actively making choices is the best way to keep our 'valves' working to preserve our mental health is important. If the complementariness of clingies and loners makes them fancy each other and form permanent (that would be nice, wouldn't it?) bonds, then the quality of those relationships, the degree to which we all accept limitations and difficulty instead of hopelessly fantasising about impossible perfections is surely up to us? In the end, being happier is about getting on with life in a positive and thoughtful way, sensitive to our own needs, those of our partners and children, and ultimately those of the larger community of which we form such a small part. Will we manage to do better than we have?

Notes

1. Quoted in Boswell, *A Tour of the Hebrides* (Harmondsworth: Penguin, 1984 [1786]), p. 266.
2. Betty Edwards, *Drawing on the Right Side of the Brain* (London: Fontana, 1982 [1979]).
3. The first draft for this section follows, illustrating how far things are seen from your own point of view even when you think you're trying to be 'objective'. It's pretty clear that this personality is difficult for me! 'A negative active loner man is a shark: he wants to have fun, and doesn't mind when his fun is bought at other people's expense. He thinks everyone should be able to look after themselves as he can, and that if everyone was strong, no-one would feel threatened.'
4. A Freudian therapist, or anyone used to 'historical' explanations of adult behaviour, would be quick, and in my view probably right, to explain such patterns by reference to potty training: the child's remembered urge to give his Mummy absolutely everything in order to postpone the time at which the inevitable fall from grace (the unwanted next poo) arrives, seems a fairly clear source for this kind of obsession with completeness for its own sake.
5. David Hume, *Enquiries concerning Human Understanding* (ed., L.A. Selby Bigge, 3rd edn. rev. P.H. Nidditch; Oxford: Clarendon Press, 1975 [1777]), p. 221.
6. Norman Bryson, *Word and Image, French Painting of the Ancien Régime* (Cambridge: Cambridge University Press, 1981).
7. *Wordsworth & Coleridge Lyrical Ballads 1798* (ed. W.J.B. Owen; London: Oxford University Press, 1969).
8. Richard Bandler and John Grinder, *Frogs into Princes: Neuro Linguistic Programming* (Moab, UT: Real People Press, 1979).
9. R.D. Laing, *The Divided Self: An Existential Study in Sanity and Madness* (Harmondsworth: Penguin, 1965 [1960]).
10. Carl Rogers, *Freedom to Learn for the 80's* (Columbus, OH: Charles E. Merrill, 1983 [lst ed. 1969]).
11. Whether this pattern arises from what we learn within the family (as a part of œdipal rivalry wanting to get Mum or Dad out of the way so that you can have better access to the parent you get on with best) or whether the family rivalry is compounded when like personalities take up œdipal roles they would have in any circumstances, is something we might look at carefully.
12. Martin Heidegger, *Being and Time* (trans., J. Macquarrie and E. Robinson; Oxford: Basil Blackwell, 1962 [1926]).